A LANDOWNER'S GUIDE TO
Western Water Rights

MARY ELLEN WOLFE

This book provides a general overview of
western water rights and law. Laws and rules
are unique to each western state and may
change yearly, so information in this guide
is likely to become outdated. We therefore
recommend consultation with an attorney
and an appropriate state agency before you
take any action regarding your water rights.
Nothing stated herein should be substituted
for professional legal advice. The author, The
Watercourse, project sponsors, and publishers
assume no liability for action taken based
upon the information contained herein.

Produced by The Watercourse

ROBERTS RINEHART PUBLISHERS
Boulder, Colorado

D1617375

First edition funded by
the U.S. Department of the Interior,
Bureau of Reclamation

ISBN 1-57098-093-4
LC # 96-067082

Produced by
The Watercourse
201 Culbertson Hall
Montana State University
Bozeman, Montana 59717
406.994.5392 office
406.994.1919 fax

Published by
Roberts Rinehart Publishers
5455 Spine Road
Boulder, Colorado 80301
303.530.4400

Distributed in the U.S. and Canada by
Publishers Group West

COVER PHOTO: Bat Lake, Medora Refuge,
northern Colorado.

MARY ELLEN WOLFE,
Program Director of The Montana
Watercourse, has over twenty years
of experience as a classroom civics
teacher, public policy educator, and
water policy analyst.

The Watercourse Staff

Dennis Nelson, Director

Sandra Robinson, Assistant Director

Gina Morrison, WETnet Coordinator

Linda Hveem, Business Manager

George Robinson, Technical Assistant
to the Director

Alan Kesselheim, Project Leader/Writer

Mary Ellen Wolfe, Program Director,
Montana Watercourse

Susan Higgins, Project Manager

John Etgen, Program Coordinator,
Project WET Montana

Contents

Acknowledgments

A Landowner's Guide to Western Water Rights has been prepared with the advice and guidance of many water education and water rights experts. The direction and support of Dennis Nelson, Director of The Watercourse, were essential for bringing this work into being. The creative suggestions of writer Sandra Robinson, Assistant Director of The Watercourse, were absolutely critical to developing a friendly and accessible publication. The substantive contributions of Mike McLane, Water Planner and former Regional Office Manager for the Montana Department of Natural Resources and Conservation, led to the creation of Parts I and III of the guide. Without Mike's help these sections would not exist. I express special thanks to John E. Thorson, Special Master of the Arizona General Stream Adjudication, who took time from his very full schedule to carefully review and comment on the publication.

Many state water rights experts also gave their time to review and comment on each western state's profile in Part IV. Sincere thanks are extended to: Gary J. Prokosch, Division of Mining and Water Management, Alaska Department of Natural Resources; Robert Nauheim, Office of the Attorney General, Alaska; Ramsey Laursoo Kropf, Office of the Special Master, Arizona General Stream Adjudication; O.P. Gulati, California State Water Resources Control Board; Joseph (Jody) Grantham, Colorado State Engineer's Office; Glen Saxton, Chief, Water Allocation Bureau, Idaho Department of Water Resources; Constance C. Owen, Assistant Legal Counsel, Kansas Division of Water Resources; Larry Holman, Chief, Water Rights Division, Montana Department of Natural Resources and Conservation; Don Blankenau, Attorney, Nebraska Water Resources Department; Naomi Dueer, State Water Planner, Nevada Division of Water Planning; R. Michael Turnipseed,

Nevada State Engineer; Hugh Ricci, Deputy State Engineer, Nevada, and Valerie Whorton, Analyst, Nevada Division of Water Resources; Robert Q. Rogers, New Mexico State Engineer's Office; Julie Krenz, Assistant Attorney General, North Dakota State Water Commission; Ms. Lou Klaver, Attorney, Oklahoma Water Resources Board; Reed Marbut, Manager, Adjudications Section, and Darlene P. Castle, Office Specialist, Oregon Water Resources Department; John Hatch, Chief Engineer, Eric Gronlund and Ron Duvall of the South Dakota Department of Environment and Natural Resources; Lann Bookout, Watershed Management, Texas Natural Resource Conservation Commission; Tony Bagwell, Director, Water Resources Planning, and David Messey, Assistant Water Plan Manager, Texas Water Development Board; Jerry Olds, Assistant State Engineer, Utah Department of Natural Resources; Kenneth Slattery, Senior Policy Analyst, Water Resources Program,

Washington Department of Ecology; John Barnes, Wyoming State Engineer's Office; Frank Carr, Administrator, Wyoming State Board of Control; and Carolyn Minder, Staff Attorney, Snake River Basin Adjudication.

Chris MacRae, Research Assistant for The Watercourse, located and acquired most of the historical photos throughout this publication and handled necessary research.

Preface

Water adjudication, prior appropriation, water transfers, beneficial use, water permits, public interest criteria, reserved water rights, instream flows, ground water recharge, return flows, and abandonment of a water right—to many western landowners, the terminology of water rights is mysterious. To more westerners than might admit, it is virtually meaningless. The complexity of water rights laws and rules makes the language daunting to the average landowner.

Western water users nevertheless increasingly encounter water rights terms in the news, in the mail, or in discussions with neighbors along the streams and the rivers in their neighborhoods. Many may have already searched for the meaning of such terms. Some may have learned a bit when a new land purchase brought a water right with it. Unfortunately, too many others learn water rights terminology the hard way—when a dispute with a neighbor leads them to a public hearing or a court of law.

A Landowner's Guide to Western Water Rights addresses many important questions by examining the terrain and essential terminology of western water rights from a broad perspective. In this book you will find answers to the following questions:

• What is a water right? When do you need one? Why should you apply for one?

• Why is the West so preoccupied with water rights?

• What different systems are used to allocate water in the United States?

• What makes the western water rights system so special?

• What is a general stream adjudication? In which western states are adjudications being conducted?

• What are reserved water rights? How are they special?

• In what ways are western states' water rights systems similar? How is each one unique?

This guide offers a friendly opportunity for the landowner to become informed about the "mysteries" of western water rights. It will serve as a reference tool for landowners, realtors, planners, elected officials, and citizens who are interested in understanding the fundamentals of water allocation in the western United States.

One important caution must be expressed. Because each state's water laws and rules are different and subject to yearly changes and judicial decisions, some information will probably become outdated. This guide is no substitute for legal advice.

Changing water laws reflect changes in the western landscape. Population growth in urban areas challenges the long-standing tendency to allocate water for agricultural use. Increasing public use of the sizable federal land-holdings in the West reveals the region's growing importance as an outdoor recreation haven for the entire nation. Additionally, powerful interests—the federal government and Native American tribes—are staking claim to long-standing western water rights. Unfortunately, these shifts inevitably run against the grain of deeply rooted western values and local rural traditions.

Competition and conflict among western water users are nothing new. The change is the ever-larger number of people who are settling, using, and having an impact on western water supplies. As a result, water rights education has become a necessity for many landowners and water users in the West. Individuals who are considering acquiring western land need to be aware that a water right may or may not automatically come with their land. Those who have recently acquired western land and are considering constructing a small pond or halting long-standing irrigation of their land need to know what procedures are required by their state—before, during, and in some cases after such activities are complete. Most important, individuals who know they own a water right need to be well informed so that they may manage the privilege they possess with care.

Water in the West:
An Introduction to the Past

Aridity and aridity alone,

makes the various wests, one.

—Wallace Stegner, *Where the Bluebird Sings to the Lemonade Springs*

"Frane LaDuke sod house, Custer County, Nebraska, 1888 or 89."
Solomon D. Butcher Collection, Nebraska State Historical Society.

Early Memories of a Prairie Homestead (late 1800s)

Always we were handicapped by a lack of water. Father's first well, dug nearly eighty feet down, bore nothing but dust. So our thirst sent us searching for water. At last, we dug a shallow well in a coulee several miles away. We traveled there daily for our water supply, which we carried home in large barrels. We stinted our water carefully for bathing, and washed our clothes in a small washbasin, since we had insufficient to fill the washtub!

When Father, Mr. Ronan and Fred began to make a small garden plot, they found that even the ground was reluctant to yield to their efforts. They spent days trying to level a space near the house. The sod was so tough it refused to be ploughed. Generations of prairie grass left roots so dense and intertwined that only a few furrows could be dug at a time.

I helped Mother with the planting and we found the job equally discouraging. The dry chunks of sod left little loose soil to cover the seeds. We were forced to pound each clod, piece by piece, to get dirt to tamp over our seeds. Mother tried to hide it, but I'm sure I saw her shed tears. Then that summer was a long and dry one. No rains came, and the heat seared the landscape. We hauled what water we could to our little garden, but only the beans grew at all. Truly, our first homestead garden was a sorry affair!

Why Is the West So Preoccupied with Water Rights?

Eastern observers of western water allocation may be puzzled by the seeming obsession of their western cousins with this issue. After all, they might argue, the United States is one country. Why are westerners so preoccupied with water? The answer is both simple and complex.

Geography lays the matter out, plain and simple. From about the ninety-eighth meridian of longitude west to the Pacific coast, average annual rainfall dips significantly below the twenty inches that normally sustain nonirrigated crops in the East. Scarcity generates westerners' preoccupation with water and water rights.

Though water scarcity in the West is common, the human habits, laws, and institutions that arose to cope with it are complex. To a considerable degree, this complexity is a reflection of the exacting years of hard labor and expense incurred by those who survived the stringent conditions of the western climate.

Hard Lessons in an
Unfamiliar Land

Condemned by many as a Great Desert, it [the West] presented a particularly stubborn obstacle to America's continental expansion because of its climate and vegetation. Americans were used to something better, and it was with considerable disappointment and apprehension that they confronted the Plains frontier.

—David M. Emmons, *Garden in the Grasslands*

Idaho State Historical Society #80-88.10.

In the beginning, there was no complex "western" water rights system. Newcomers to the arid West confronted unfamiliar circumstances. The fur trappers, traders, miners, and finally farmers and ranchers met a land that challenged the best in them. And they faced evidence of the dry western climate in more than a lack of rainfall and dry air. The very forms of the western landscape—buttes, coulees, badlands, prairies, arroyos, mesas, canyons—were geologic testimony to the awesome forces that would shape their own lives in the West.

Onto the open public lands the settlers came and immediately went to work. Just about everything they did required water: sluicing mining operations; soaking bone-dry fields; watering thirsty cattle, sheep, and gardens— almost everything involved in developing the land. At first, no laws constrained settlers' activities. It was left to nature to suggest or to impose new ways of doing things. The western rookies had sobering lessons to learn.

Settlers in the northern regions of the West didn't know that centuries before them (500 B.C.), the Hohokam people of the desert Southwest had constructed irrigation canals and diversions from the Gila River. Nor were they aware that irrigation had provided the economic foundation for the Pueblo people in New Mexico well before the Spanish settlements in the 1500s.[1]

Unlike people settling the arid regions of the West that became Texas, New Mexico, Arizona, and southern California, newcomers to the central and northern plains and prairies, the Rocky Mountains, and the Pacific Northwest encountered no long-standing irrigation systems. They relied on their own resourcefulness and hard-earned knowledge to survive the unfamiliar climatic circumstances.

Settlers learned to dig ditches and canals to bring scarce water to mining operations. They learned to irrigate and to dig the laterals necessary to convey water to land distant from streams and rivers. They learned to construct diversion dams and, later, **reservoirs**, to store floodwaters for dry times. They learned it was all hard work and expensive. Inevitably, they developed ways to protect their investments. In large part, the water rights systems in each of the western states today are the fruit of these early labors.

Luckily for western water users, many states copied one another when the need arose about the time of statehood to create individual state water rights systems. As a result, several general attributes characterize all western water rights systems.

This guide describes these common attributes for the landowner and the layperson. Part I investigates "The

Most Frequently Asked Questions about Western Water Rights." Part II, "Navigating Western Water Rights: A Reference Guide," provides an overview of western water rights (Chapter One), followed by more specific details regarding the prior appropriation system (Chapter Two), federal reserved water rights (Chapter Two), and the prospects for western water rights in the future (Chapter Three). Part III then offers "Cautions for New and Potential Landowners." Part IV, "Profiles of Western States' Water Rights Systems," offers direction to appropriate state water rights agencies and summarizes key attributes of each state's water rights system. The guide concludes with a Glossary of water terms and References.

How might this guide be used? Newcomers to western water rights might find Part I to be the best starting point. Novices may find a short answer there for questions foremost in their minds. Beginners are cautioned, however. Water rights are grounded in complex legal principles developed and defined within each individual western state. As a result, short answers may be deceiving. To minimize this problem, each short answer points to more detailed information elsewhere in this book. The reader is directed to possible outside information sources as well.

Those more experienced in western water rights may also find Part I to be informative. However, those already familiar with the fundamentals may begin with the more lengthy (though still greatly abbreviated) details of the prior appropriation system (Part II, Chapter Two) or review their state's water rights system profile (Part IV). Some readers may even be interested in browsing through the individual state profiles to see how their state's approach to water rights resembles others.

Navigating western water rights can be a challenge. Yet those who are curious and persistent may be amazed at their ability to acquire a basic understanding of water rights concepts that they believed were exclusive to experts and attorneys. Read on! Your discovery tour into western water rights has just begun!

*Note: Words **bold-faced** at first use are found in the Glossary; quotation marks are used for terms defined in context.*

PART I
The Most Frequently
Asked Questions about
Western Water Rights

"Irrigation well Tri-County area, Charles G.
Wallace of Hastings, Nebraska at right."
Nebraska State Historical Society.

What is a water right?

Basically, a **water right** is a right to use a public resource for a beneficial purpose. Water rights are considered **property rights,** but private persons can't actually own water.

Are water rights for a well the same as water rights to a stream or river?

Most western states define **surface water** and **ground water** rights separately and distinctly. Individual state laws and rights related to surface water and ground water are also likely to differ accordingly.

See Chapter Two, "Prior Appropriation: What's It All About?"—particularly "What Is a Water Right?" and "How Does the Prior Appropriation System Work?" Also see your state's profile in Part IV to identify your state agency contact for water rights. Your attorney may be another important contact.

Who needs a water right?

Anyone diverting and controlling water in a western state needs or should already have a water right. Private water rights holders may include irrigators, municipal water suppliers, municipal wells, and commercial and industrial operations. Urban residents who use water supplied by a public agency generally receive their water by virtue of the municipal water supplier's water right.

What is a diversion?

A **diversion** is a structure used to capture water before it is put to use. Examples include pumps, irrigation headgates, ditches, pipelines, and dams. Individual states commonly define diversions by law.

See Chapter Two, "Prior Appropriation: What's It All About?"—particularly "How Does the Prior Appropriation System Work?"

What is a consumptive use of water?

Irrigation, private domestic wells, fish raceways and ponds, and stock water ponds are all examples of diversionary, **consumptive uses** of water. Consumptive water use means that some part of the water diverted is consumed, making at least a portion unavailable for use by others.

See "How Does the Prior Appropriation System Work?" in Chapter Two.

What is an instream (or nonconsumptive) use of water?

Instream water uses may include water for hydropower production, fisheries and wildlife habitat, water quality protection, and stream channel protection. Some states have adopted laws and regulations that provide a measure of protection for these **nonconsumptive** uses.

See Chapter One, "What's So Special about Western Water Rights? An Overview," particularly "Instream Flow Rights: What Are They?"

Alhambra Hot Springs.
Montana Historical Society, Helena.

Why do I need a new water right?

A water right gives you legal standing to assert your water use against conflicting water users who do not have water rights. Furthermore:

• Water rights give their holders a priority to use water over persons with a later priority or those who filed later for water rights from the same source. The rights are a way to protect the water user's investment, whether it is an irrigation project or a domestic well.

• Anyone who diverts, impounds, or withdraws water or uses a significant amount of water without the proper state permit or certificate may be violating state law. Potentially this might involve liabilities such as fines, penalties, and even the payment of damages to other water rights holders.

• Having a water right allows a user to **call the river** and enter into water use agreements with others. (See below for more on making call and water use agreements.)

• A water right is a property right to use a public resource; possessing one therefore may increase the economic value of a landowner's property.

• A person who files for a water right provides valuable information to the state and other water users about water use and water availability. This information allows state water managers to

• estimate present uses of water

• determine how much water is available

• protect priority water rights holders

• prevent overappropriation of water sources

• better manage states' water resources in the future

• Because all water rights should be officially recorded, it is possible to use your state's records to identify and locate other water rights holders using the same watercourse.

See Chapter Two, "Prior Appropriation: What's It All About?"

How is a water right established?

To establish a right under the prior appropriation system in the past, water had only to be put to **beneficial use.** In the modern era, new water rights are established through state-specific processes that generally begin with making application and filing for a permit.

See Chapter One, "What's So Special About Western Water Rights: An Overview," particularly "Prior Appropriation: A System for the Situation," for a summary answer and brief historical description of the origins of prior appropriation. For further detail, see Chapter Two, "Prior Appropriation: What's It All About?" In addition, see your state's profile to obtain a general idea about how your state establishes water rights. Finally, contact the appropriate state agency and/or your attorney.

What is the prior appropriation system?

The **prior appropriation system,** also known as the **appropriation** or **prior appropriation doctrine,** is a widely used method for allocating water in the West to many uses and needs. It rests on the principle of "priority," or "first in time, first in right." That is, whoever began using water first (a so-called senior) has the right of first use. Furthermore, the senior user is entitled to his/her full amount before those with subsequent (or junior) water rights receive their share.

See previous response.

What is beneficial use?

Generally, beneficial use is water used for some "good" purpose, usually defined specifically within state law. Traditional legal definitions usually include domestic, municipal, agricultural (irrigation and stock water), and industrial uses (mining, etc.). Some states also include hydropower, fish and wildlife, recreation, navigation, public parks, game preserves, and so on.

See Chapter Two, "Prior Appropriation: What's It All About?"—particularly "How Does the Prior Appropriation System Work?" The most complete answer to this question will be obtained from the agency listed in your state's profile in Part IV, state law, or your attorney.

How do I get a water right?

If you are already diverting and using water, you may already have a valid water right. If water was used on your property before you owned it, and you have continued to use it, you may have gotten a water right with your land. Contact the appropriate state water management agency that maintains water rights records to find out if you have a water right.

You will need to obtain a new water right for a new water use or if you discover that your existing use wasn't properly established. New water rights are initiated by first making application to the appropriate state agency.

In most western states, before water laws were adopted, putting water to beneficial use was sufficient to establish a water right. After water codes were created, new water rights were established by filing an application with the appropriate state agency. Filing application for a water right is usually the first step in a series of steps, instituted differently by each western state. Making application may or may not culminate in the issuance of a new water permit.

See your state's profile in Part IV and contact the appropriate agency for further information and detail. See "How Are Water Rights Obtained?" in Chapter Two, "Prior Appropriation: What's It All About?" for a general description of state procedures. For an overview of the details of your state's procedure, see the appropriate state profile in Part IV. For the most complete information, contact the responsible agency listed in your state's profile.

Who should I contact to get a water right?

Each state has its own procedures for allocating new water rights. Generally, authority for this task rests with a water management agency, such as the Department of Water Resources or Department of Natural Resources or state engineer.

See previous response.

What is a water permit?

The term **water permit** generally refers to a water right that has not become final (or become **vested, perfected**, or **certificated**). This means that although the terms and conditions of an approved application for a water right have not yet been fulfilled, permission has been granted to use water or develop a water project or facility until the terms and conditions are accomplished.

See "How Does the Prior Appropriation System Work?" and "How Are Water Rights Obtained?" in Chapter Two, "Prior Appropriation: What's It All About?" For the most complete answer, contact the appropriate agency in your state, listed in Part IV.

Helena, Montana, fire, July 16, 1928.
Montana State Historical Society.

Are there limits to my water right?

Water rights under the prior appropriation doctrine extend only to water that is beneficially used. They do not extend to water that is wasted or used inefficiently. Because wasteful practices can involve sizable water losses, some states apply specified limitations on the amount or rate of water that can be diverted and/or used. Limits on the amount of water are often called the **duty of water** and are based on a reasonable assumption of the quantity of water (e.g., average, maximum) that would be required for a specified use or purpose in a given area.

See Chapter Two, particularly "Do Limits Exist to Appropriation Rights?"

I have several shares in an irrigation company. Does this mean that I have a water right?

Not necessarily. The irrigation company owns the water right and you, as a shareholder, have an interest in the company. As a shareholder, you do have some rights and privileges, but the company has the water right. The issue of who owns the water right can raise questions during land transfers. For example, in Utah, when land with an associated water right is transferred from one owner to another, and the deed is silent regarding the water rights, existing rights automatically transfer with the land. However, if land is sold by an owner who was a shareholder in an irrigation company, the shares of stock do not transfer with the land.

Answers to this question may differ with each state. See your state's profile and contact the proper state agency for complete information.

I'm a new landowner. Who should I contact to find out if a water right is attached to my land?

If you are a landowner in a town or city, you probably obtain your water from a public supplier. In such cases, the municipality probably has the water right, and you are provided with a supply of water as a paid public service. If you are a new suburban or rural landowner, your realtor or title company should have informed you about a water right attached to your land purchase, well before the transaction occurred. Usually, if land with an attached water right is conveyed to a new owner, the water right transfers automatically with the land deed. Some states allow for a water right to be "severed" or "detached" from the land. This commonly involves a written deed or contract specifying how this will occur. Most western states require that some formal paperwork be filed with the appropriate state water management agency showing that a change in ownership or location of the water right has occurred.

Each state's answer to this question will probably differ somewhat, so see your state's profile to identify the agency contact you should make to get the complete answer to this question. For additional cautions, see Part III, which provides some helpful water rights hints for the landowner.

What should I do if I have a water right, but there is no water available to tap?

Contact the appropriate state water management agency to learn who can help you address this problem. In some cases, you may need to identify the local person who oversees water allocation in your local area (for example, a **water commissioner, ditch rider,** or **mayordomo**). You will need to find out what your priority date is and perhaps the priority dates of others drawing water from the same source. Once this is accomplished, you may be able to call the river and force junior water rights holders to cease their water use until you receive your full, legal share.

See your state's profile in Part IV to identify the agency contact you should make to get the most appropriate and complete answer to this question for your local area.

What is "making call"?

When a senior water user **makes call** (or calls the river), he/she asks for enforcement of the priority ranking of water rights for the relevant portion of the river or stream. This typically requires that a responsible public official (for example, a water commissioner or state engineer) enforce the priority system. This may involve requesting junior water users to cease water use until seniors' full water entitlements have been satisfied.

See your state's profile in Part IV to identify the agency contact you should make to get the most appropriate and complete answer to this question for your local area.

What is a "water use agreement"?

A water use agreement can be a mutually developed, formal written understanding between all water users on a given stream to allocate the water in a particular way (for example, sharing water shortages rather than strictly enforcing the legal priority ranking). A water use agreement may also be informal, such as a verbal commitment to repair a leaky irrigation canal. Water use agreements have the advantage of being developed by water users and for water users. They can provide flexibility in water use that strict adherence to the prior appropriation system might not allow. For example, the state of Oregon encourages the use of "rotational agreements." These commonly involve agreements to share water and make better use of it, regardless of the senior/junior water rights hierarchy. Check with the proper state water management agency to learn if such agreements are ever used in your state.

See previous response.

May I change my water right?

Yes. Although states vary, most western states allow for the point of diversion, place of use, period of use, time of use, or nature of use of a water right to be changed as long as doing so doesn't harm others. States generally require that a water rights holder make application with the appropriate water rights management agency before making any change.

Most western states consider water rights to be "appurtenant" to the land on which they are used. This means that when land is sold, water rights that are attached to the land automatically transfer with the sale. Some states allow for a water right to be severed from the land, or sold separately, but this is accomplished by a separate deed.

See "May a Water Right Be Changed?" in Chapter Two for a general answer. For details of your state's procedure, identify the appropriate state agency contact listed in your state's profile in Part IV.

"Irrigating from the Yellowstone River, MT." 1894. Haynes Foundation Collection, Montana Historical Society, Helena, Montana.

May I transfer my water right?

Each individual state has its own laws and procedures for transferring water rights, and considerable differences may exist among them.

See "May a Water Right Be Transferred?" in Chapter Two for a general answer. For details of your state's procedure, identify the appropriate state agency contact listed in your state's profile in Part IV.

Can I lose my water right?

Yes. Water rights under the prior appropriation system can be lost if they are not used. Particular time periods are usually defined in each state's water law and accompanied by special procedures for determining that a water right has been **abandoned** or **forfeited.** States may deem a water right has been abandoned if it is determined that a water right was not used, intentionally, for a specified period of time. A water right may be forfeited, unintentionally, by failure to put it to use for a specified time period.

See "Can a Water Right Be Lost?" in Chapter Two for a brief answer. Also examine your state's profile in Part IV. Contact your attorney and/or the appropriate state agency for more complete information regarding your water right and your state's procedures.

What are federal reserved water rights?

The term **reserved rights** refers to the special water rights that belong to the federal government or Native American tribes and reservations. These rights have been developed differently from state prior appropriation water rights to provide water to satisfy the purposes for which federal and tribal lands were set aside. (Federal reserved water rights are not to be confused with **water reservations** established in some states' laws.)

For an overview, see "Federal Reserved Water Rights" and "Federal and State Water Rights: How Do They Differ?" in Chapter One. For more detail, see "What Are Federal and Tribal Reserved Water Rights?" in Chapter Two and your state's profile in Part IV.

How do state water rights differ from federal water rights?

Federal reserved water rights are fundamentally different from water rights granted by state authorities. They differ according to (1) the source from which they derive (federal treaty, law, or executive order), (2) the basis of the right (the purpose of the reservation of land), (3) the priority date (date the land was set aside), and (4) the quantity of water involved (the amount necessary to fulfill the purpose for which the land was reserved). Unlike water rights acquired through state law, federal reserved water rights cannot be forfeited by nonuse.

See Table One in the section "Federal and State Water Rights: How Do They Differ?" in Chapter One.

Water rights seem to only involve water quantity. What about water quality? Is there any relationship between the two?

Traditionally, western states have managed water quantity and water quality separately. However, in many parts of the West the increased demand for water has coincided with degradation resulting from water use, making it clear that water quality and quantity are integral to one another. As a result, many western states are taking steps to integrate their water management and planning to account for both water quantity and water quality concerns. Some states now include water quality criteria when considering new appropriations of water.

See Chapter Three, "What's the Prospect for Western Water Rights in the Twenty-first Century?" and your state's profile in Part IV.

How is ground water allocated?

Ground water is allocated according to individual states' laws and regulations. Some states have permitting processes for new ground water uses. Some states base ground water use on ownership of overlying lands. In some states, ground water users whose right predates others are protected from harmful effects of subsequent users. Most states recognize ground water as a public resource that is subject to management under state authority.

See "Ground Water Rights: How Do They Differ from Surface Water Rights?" in Chapter One.

What is the "public trust doctrine"?

The public trust is a long-standing doctrine dating back to Roman civil law and English common law. It obligates government (as sovereign) to protect special and common resources of public importance. It has been applied to protect public uses of water and to ensure access to **navigable waters** for passage, commerce, and fisheries. The doctrine has been applied in specific court cases. *Illinois Central Railroad v. Illinois* and *National Audubon Society v. Superior Court*, known as the Mono Lake decision, are two important examples.

See "Do Limits Exist to Appropriation Rights?" in Chapter Two.

What are public interest criteria?

Most western states have significantly enhanced the protection of "public interest values," which are considered during their water-permitting processes. State courts and state legislatures across the West have identified public interest criteria (sometimes called "public welfare" criteria) that must be considered and met when an application to appropriate water or transfer a right is under consideration. Specific public interest criteria differ from state to state. Some examples include benefits to the applicant from the proposed activity, effect on economic activity, effect on fish and game and public recreation opportunities, public health effects, harm to other persons, and other such public interest considerations.

See "How Are Water Rights Obtained?" in Chapter Two and "What's the Public Interest?" in Chapter Three. Also see your state's profile in Part IV.

What is a general stream adjudication?

A general stream **adjudication** is a special kind of judicial proceeding that determines the type, the amount, and the priority date of every water user's water right in a particular watershed. The intent is usually to verify and clarify the nature and extent of the competing water rights of all water users in a particular stream or river system.

Individual states' adjudication processes differ. For example, Oregon's adjudication is a process to verify and document vested water rights that are not of record. These involve water uses made before Oregon's water codes were adopted in 1909, which include federal water claims and federal water rights.

See "General Stream Adjudications in the West Today" in Chapter One.

"Home of the River Crows."
Montana Historical Society, Helena.

PART II
Navigating
Western Water Rights:
A Reference Guide

The life of the law is not logic, but experience.

—*Oliver Wendell Holmes*

Idaho State Historical Society 63-183.5.

Excerpt from a Prospector's Diary: Staking a Claim

May 30th. All is well. Bill spotted a piece of rimrock over yonder and we prospected there all day. Bill dug the dirt and filled the pan. I carried it to the creek and washed it. I whirled it around and seen that we had some good dirt. Bill found a scad. When we weighed it, we had four dollars and eighty cents!

May 31st. Riley, Cap and Ben gave our spot a try today. They beat Bill and me up early and got more gold by noon than me and Bill did before. We panned turns most of the day. One hundred and fifty dollars of good dust!

June 1st. We staked the ground first thing. Claimed one hundred feet. Riley wanted a water right too—a sign posted for a water right. He asked me to write it for him. I did but asked him, "What name shall we give this creek?" The boys said, "You name it." So I wrote "Muddy" cause it was. Then we staked eight claims for our friends and named them all too. We agreed not to tell no one of what we had found, but to prospect the gulch well and get the best.

CHAPTER ONE:

WHAT'S SO SPECIAL ABOUT WESTERN WATER RIGHTS?

AN OVERVIEW

The novice interested in learning more about water rights in the western United States—whether a new landowner, someone contemplating a land purchase, a realtor, county planner, elected official, or other interested citizen—is well advised to begin with the basics. A brief overview of fundamentals—prior appropriation, hybrid systems, federal and Indian water rights, ground water rights, general stream adjudications, and instream flow water rights—will lay a useful foundation for the more detailed look in Part IV at each western state's water rights system.

The Eastern Tradition: Riparian Rights

East of the ninety-eighth meridian, rainfall and watercourses are abundant, and water rights belong to those who own "riparian" lands—property along a stream, river, or other watercourse. **Riparian rights** entitle such landowners to make "reasonable use" of water on their riparian lands, defined as a use that doesn't interfere with the reasonable use of other riparian landowners. Riparian rights also include

• a right of access to the watercourse

• a right to fish

• a right to unpolluted water

• a right to prevent erosion of the stream bank[2]

Taken together, these rights constitute **riparian doctrine**.

In contrast, western water rights were developed for the circumstances and needs of nineteenth-century settlers. They evolved from the customs and practices of miners, who, beginning with the discovery of gold on the American River in California in 1848, developed systems for protecting their claims to land and minerals.

The customs and rules the miners established defined the nature of property rights on their claims to land. Several of their practices for staking claims to minerals also were used to allocate western waters:

• A notice of claim was to be posted and officially recorded.

• To remain valid, a claim had to be worked with diligence, or it could be lost (forfeited).

• Where questions of right to a mineral claim arose, they were resolved on the basis of "first in time, first in right."

It was only a matter of time before mineral claims gave way to water claims (primarily for surface water). When this happened, the same three principles were applied. Whoever diverted water first had the prior right to use it. To secure the right, ditches were to be dug "with diligence" (concerted, observable effort or action). And the water had to be put to a beneficial use. Furthermore, when and if a water use ceased, so did the right. These became the principles of the prior appropriation doctrine.

We would think it very strange of any man who would pay a high price for a thoroughbred and not demand the papers with the horse. The papers do not make the thoroughbred a better horse, but they do make him far more valuable to the owner and more interesting to others. History is the "papers" of man; it is the register of his lineage, the record of his performance, and the guarantee of his qualities.

—Walter Prescott Webb, *History as High Adventure*

Prior Appropriation:
A System for the Situation

The Prior Appropriation Doctrine evolved to protect and reward those who risked the effort and invested the financial resources to develop the arid western lands. In contrast to eastern conditions, natural circumstances in much of the West made the use of riparian water law unworkable. For one, early miners did not own the lands they prospected; they were trespassers on public lands. Second, mining claims were often far from water. To successfully extract ores, large quantities of water sometimes had to be brought from a distant water source. Had a riparian system been established, with water use requiring ownership of the lands along a watercourse, much mineral extraction in the West would have been impossible. The same circumstances held true for homesteaders.

The federal government was responsible for opening the public lands to later prospectors and homesteaders through a succession of land laws. The 1866 Mining Act (and its 1870 amendment) and the 1877 Desert Land Act recognized the importance of evolving local custom and established the legitimacy of the emerging state-based prior appropriation systems. The laws came at a good time. Thousands of acres of public land were essentially worthless without water, and streams and rivers in the West were few and frequently intermittent. Early homesteaders learned quickly that sizable investments must be made—canals dug, laterals laid, stock ponds constructed, and eventually dams and reservoirs built—to provide a reliable water supply.

The prior appropriation system provided the guarantees that westerners required. Anyone could divert whatever quantity of water was desired to any distance they could reach. Whoever applied water first had the first right to use it. Thus, holding senior water rights was (and remains) preferable to, and more secure than, possessing junior rights.

Willow Creek Dam. The Northeastern Nevada Museum, Elko. #173-26[p. 30].

The One-Armed Visionary

Any story of western water rights is incomplete without mention of the great explorer of western rivers, John Wesley Powell, who wrote: "A thousand millions of money must be used; who shall furnish it? Great and many industries are to be established; who shall control them? Millions of men are to labor; who shall employ them? This is a great nation, the Government is powerful; shall it engage in this work? . . . I say to the Government: Hands off! Furnish the people with institutions of justice, and let them do the work for themselves."

The "Hybrid" Approach

Over time, not every western state chose to rely solely on prior appropriation to allocate water. The eight driest did: Arizona, Colorado, Idaho, Montana, Nevada, New Mexico, Utah, and Wyoming. Several other states instituted a combination of riparian and prior appropriation practices in statute and case law. Because California was the first to do so, **hybrid systems** such as these are sometimes said to follow the California Doctrine. Most western states have since limited or invalidated the scope of previously recognized riparian rights. Ten states have created permit or appropriation systems that modify or replace riparian rights.

Federal Reserved Water Rights

The challenge of understanding water rights in the western United States today is compounded by the existence of federal and tribal reserved water rights. These rights are separate and different from the state-based water appropriation rights acquired under the prior appropriation doctrine and from hybrid systems.

Federal and Indian reserved water rights have been created to provide adequate water for lands owned by the federal government and Native American tribes. The Federal Reserved Rights Doctrine acknowledges rights to a quantity of water sufficient to fulfill the purposes for which land was set aside. Unlike state rights allocated under the Prior Appropriation Doctrine, reserved rights on federal and tribal land do not have to be used to be valid. The priority date for federal reserved water rights is at least as early as the date land was set aside, even if others used water earlier from the same source. Furthermore, federal and tribal reserved rights are not generally subject to state law.[3]

Federal and State Water Rights: How Do They Differ?

A useful way to understand state appropriative water rights and federal reserved water rights is to compare them according to (1) their source of origin, (2) the basis of the right, (3) the date of their priority, and (4) the quantity of water the right gives authority to use. Table One clarifies the considerable differences between federal reserved water rights and state appropriative water rights.

The basis of water rights issued by individual western states rests with the authority given to the state in laws or statutes. Contrast this with federal reserved water rights, which result from federal lands set aside by treaty, federal statutes, and executive orders of the president.

A valid water right under state appropriation systems is based on historical evidence that the water has been put to beneficial use. In contrast, federal and tribal water rights are based on the purpose for which the federal land was set aside.

Determination of the priority date associated with a state or a federal reserved water right also differs. The priority date for state appropriative rights is generally the date on which water was first put to use or the date on which the permit application was filed and accepted. The priority date for reserved water rights is the date on which the land was withdrawn from the public domain.

The quantity of water associated with a state appropriative right is either the amount used historically or the amount reasonably necessary to meet the beneficial uses. This right can be lost by nonuse. (For many years, western water users have warned one another to "use it or lose it.") Federal and Indian reserved water rights differ again. The quantity of water associated with these rights is the amount necessary to fulfill the purposes for which the land was set aside and cannot be abandoned by a failure to use water. In the case of Indian water rights, **practicably irrigable acreage** (PIA) criteria are used to determine "the amount necessary to fulfill the purposes for which the land was set aside." (See Chapter Two, pages 60–61 and Glossary for additional information.)

Table One

Federal Reserved Water Rights and State Appropriative Water Rights: A Comparison

	State Appropriative Rights	Federal Reserved Rights
SOURCE	State statutes	Federal tribal treaties, statutes, and executive orders
BASIS	Historic beneficial use	Purpose of the reservation
PRIORITY	Date first put to beneficial use	Date the land was withdrawn (or earlier aboriginal use)
QUANTITY	Historic beneficial use unless abandoned	Amount necessary to fulfill purposes for which land was reserved therefore cannot be abandoned

"On Cliff Table, putting down a deep well, 1889." Solomon D. Butcher Collection, Nebraska State Historical Society.

Ground Water Rights: How Do They Differ from Surface Water Rights?

The rights and obligations for ground water use in the western states are generally tied to two legal principles: (1) property ownership and (2) shared ownership of a public, "common pool" resource. From these two notions, a variety of state approaches to ground water rights has evolved. Most western states do not recognize private ownership rights in ground water, so ground water is managed as public property. Typically, western states have adopted ground water allocation systems that combine aspects of the above two principles. For example, a state may acknowledge ownership of ground water by an overlying landowner but restrict use to "reasonable" quantities only. And special protections may be provided for earlier users against subsequent ground water users. Also, all users from a ground water source may be protected against **aquifer** contamination.

In some western states where ground water is abundant, the allocation of rights has received little attention. However, the increasing incidence of ground water contamination has caused most states to focus more attention on ground water. The benefit of owning a ground water right usually brings with it the right to protect that source from pollution by others.

Ground water–permitting systems have been established in many western states. In some instances, state permit systems replace piecemeal ground water policy established in earlier court battles. Today, ground water–permitting systems are useful for advancing public understanding of ground water use and providing a tool for community control of pumping activity.

General Stream Adjudications in the West Today

All western states have established judicial procedures to determine the rights of water users competing for the flow of a given stream or river. Such judicial proceedings, also called adjudications, are initiated in different ways by different states—by water users, by state agencies, or by both.

Generally, adjudications are intended to be universal and a complete determination of all existing rights. Once accomplished, adjudications fulfill three important functions: (1) to create a public record of all valid water rights,[4] (2) to allow fair distribution of water,[5] and (3) to provide for planning for future water allocation.[6]

Where stream adjudications are occurring, a state agency commonly acts as information gatherer. To determine all rights in a basin or subbasin, this agency accepts and evaluates claims and conducts technical surveys and other analyses.

Thereafter, most states require that an administrative report or proposed **decree** be filed in a court of law. The court typically is charged with resolving objections to the report or proposed decree and then issuing a final decree, which describes all of the water rights in that stream system.

Appeals from interested and affected parties are allowed before the court makes its final determination of all water rights in a given stream or river.

Many western states adjudicate water rights in one or several watersheds at a time. Arizona, California, Colorado, Idaho, New Mexico, Nevada, Oregon, Texas, Washington, Wyoming, and Utah all use this technique. Montana chose to undertake a statewide stream adjudication in 1982.

Instream Flow Rights: What Are They?

Historically, the bulk of western water use has been for irrigated agriculture. The water laws that have evolved to allocate such rights have, consequently, emphasized water diversions and developments. Today, western states increasingly acknowledge the economic value and ecological benefits of keeping sufficient water in the stream. Hydropower production, recreation, water quality protection, and fish, wildlife, and habitat preservation are among the common reasons given for protecting **instream flows.**

As a result, most western states have adopted some type of legislation to protect these instream values. In general, the following techniques have been used.

Prohibitions Against New Diversions

Probably the first state to take steps to protect instream flows was Oregon, which adopted legislation in the 1920s. A moratorium was placed on new withdrawals from a number of streams deemed to have highly valued salmon fisheries and scenic beauty. California followed Oregon's example in 1972. It prohibited further diversions and dams in certain rivers and preserved their "free-flowing state" because they possessed "extraordinary scenic, recreational, fishery, or wildlife values."

Water Use Permit Denial and Conditions

All western states require that new water users file an application in order to acquire a new water right. Some states protect instream flows by applying approval criteria or **conditional-use provisions** before approving a new water right.

For example, in 1949 the state of Washington authorized state government to deny permit applications if a new use would lower the stream flow below the level "necessary to adequately support food, fish and game fish populations." Likewise, the Utah legislature decided that water permits could be denied if they unreasonably affected "public recreation or the natural stream environment."

"President Roosevelt party at the East Hill Observation Point during his second visit to Fort Peck Dam."
Montana Historical Society, Helena.

Other states such as California and Alaska have used related, but more flexible, techniques. California allows new water uses but requires that the permit holder leave a specified level of natural flow in the stream. Alaska requires that a permittee stop diverting water when the natural stream level falls below a specified level of flow.

Some states have acknowledged instream flow rights on a par with other consumptive water rights, such as municipal or irrigation diversions. These instream flow rights are established under state law using four mechanisms:

APPROPRIATION. The idea of instream appropriation dates to 1925, when the Idaho legislature designated water rights to preserve certain lakes for their scenic beauty and recreational values. The governor of the state holds these water rights in trust for the people of Idaho. In 1973, Colorado broadened the concept by adopting legislation allowing the Colorado Water Conservation Board to establish water rights for the public to maintain instream flows and lake levels. Wyoming, Hawaii, and Oregon have since set up programs similar to Colorado's.

WATER RESERVATIONS. Water reservations set aside or reserve water for future uses. Montana and Alaska have state reservation programs that include the reservation of water for instream flow purposes. In Montana, an applicant must be a political subdivision of the state or federal government, whereas Alaska allows any person or entity to seek a water reservation. Both states require substantial review before the reservation is granted, and in both states, future consumptive uses of water are not necessarily prohibited through the procedure.

TEMPORARY TRANSFERS OF SENIOR WATER RIGHTS. Overappropriation of water is a fact of life along many western waterways. Legislation in some states now allows for the acquisition and conversion of existing water rights to instream flow purposes. Utah, Wyoming, and Colorado have passed legislation that effectively grants this authority to the states.

Another mechanism being used is promotion of **temporary transfers** of water to protect instream flows during critical periods. During the 1987 drought, for example, a $20,000 purchase of ten thousand **acre-feet** of water helped the Montana Department of Fish, Wildlife and Parks to protect stream flow in the Bitterroot River.

THE PUBLIC TRUST. In some instances, instream flow rights may have been obtained and held as part of the "public trust." Public trust considerations are not a formula for granting water rights, but instead require evaluation of all public needs for water before allocation is made to one need.

This approach is supported by a growing body of case law that holds that streams, lakes, marshlands, and other water resources are part of the people's heritage and that state governments have the authority and duty to protect these resources. A number of western states have relied on public trust principles to protect aspects of their water resources: stream access in Montana; preservation of land for scientific study, habitat, and open space in California; recreation, aesthetics, water quality, and a range of wildlife habitat values in Idaho; fishing, boating, swimming and waterskiing, and related purposes in Washington; water supply, fisheries, and future needs in North Dakota; and all public resources in Hawaii.[7]

The protection of instream flow values in the West is controversial. Population growth, land development, the increasing economic importance of recreation, and water quality protection mandates are forces that press for protection of instream flows. The controversy frequently hinges on senior, consumptive water users' protests that instream flow protection will prohibit future water development. To address this concern, most western states have restricted the acquisition of instream flow water rights to state or other public ownership. But as competition for scarce resources has intensified, some individuals and groups have taken steps to transfer existing consumptive use water rights to privately held instream flow rights. Arizona has wrestled with this issue. In Alaska, this is not an issue because state residents may acquire an instream water right. Regardless of the state's approach, it is clear that instream flow issues will continue to demand attention.

This brief overview of western water rights is the basis for closer examination of the Prior Appropriation Doctrine in Chapter Two.

Powerhouse, Bonneville Dam. Photo by Brian Walsh.

CHAPTER TWO:

PRIOR APPROPRIATION:

WHAT'S IT ALL ABOUT?

What Is a Water Right?

Like trout, ducks, or wildlife, water is a public resource. Private persons can't actually *own* water, but they can own a right *to use* water. Thus a water right is considered a property right that permits the use of a certain amount of water in a certain location and in a certain way.

Idaho State Historical Society #82-114.26.

All prior appropriation states have declared that water either belongs to the public or to the state. Unlike a privately held water right, state ownership asserts sovereign interests in water rather than property interests. Generally, then, water is a public resource that is administered by states on behalf of their citizens.

Because no individual or entity can own water, states have created different laws to help them allocate private rights to use water for beneficial purposes. The private property interest of a water rights holder varies in nature from state to state. In appropriation states, the property interest is limited to a right to divert and use a certain quantity. This type of right is called a **usufructuary right**. If water is diverted for a useful purpose, the user is a custodian of the resource and has certain rights and duties in relation to other water users and the state.

How Does the Prior Appropriation System Work?

One must be careful about generalizing about the prior appropriation doctrine in all western states. It is fair to say, however, that three common devices are routinely used to determine whether a western water appropriation is valid: diversion, intent, and beneficial use. Use of these three "yardsticks" has developed over time to prevent fraud and to provide order for what began in all western states as unregulated water allocation systems. States apply these criteria to monitor water use and thereby ensure that it coincides with the public good.

D I V E R S I O N . One important device is diversion. This involves some change in all or a part of a stream or river that directs water flow away from its natural course. Methods of diversion vary but can include dams, reservoirs, ditches, canals, pumps, pipes, and flumes.

Some states require a physical diversion of water for a water appropriation to be valid. Other states allow water appropriations for uses that do not require physical structures or human acts—instream flow uses, for example.

The diversion requirement helps water managers notify existing and prospective water users that a water appropriation has been made. It also serves to give state and court authorities a basis for determining a priority date for a water appropriation. Some states use the capacity of a diversion structure to define the quantity of water to which an appropriator is entitled. States that require water permits may require due diligence in completing a diversion project before a water right is finalized.

In sum, it is not safe to generalize widely about the diversion requirement in all western states, because of the differences and exceptions that characterize its meaning and application in each individual state.

INTENT. A second important indicator of a valid water appropriation is "intent," meaning that a water user must intend to use water for some beneficial purpose. The purpose is usually determined when an application is made, along with the quantity, flow rate, point of diversion, and times when the water can be taken from its source. Proving intent can require an "open, physical demonstration" (as in Colorado) or may simply involve filing an application with the appropriate state agency to acquire a water use permit.

Willow Creek Dam.
The Northeastern Nevada Museum, Elko, #173-14.

The broad implications of the beneficial use doctrine are described by David Getches:

Once an appropriator puts water to a use considered beneficial by state law, the right is perfected. The right becomes absolute and its priority in times of shortage will not be defeated even by more socially important, economically more valuable or more efficient uses by a junior appropriator.

—*Water Law in a Nutshell*

BENEFICIAL USE. Beneficial use is the measure, the basis and the limit of the appropriator's right to use water.[8] Thus, putting water to beneficial use is perhaps the most important step in finalizing or perfecting a water right.

Beneficial uses in prior appropriation states include domestic, municipal, agricultural, and industrial uses. However, many states define beneficial uses more specifically.

The definition of beneficial uses has evolved historically, from quite limited uses in the past—domestic, irrigation, stock, and mining—to recreation and even scenic or aesthetic uses in some western states today.

Some states have adopted **preference systems** that rank types of water use according to relative importance. Most of these identify domestic or municipal purposes as the highest use, agriculture as second, and industrial and mining third.

Preference laws have rarely been used during times of shortage to require that preferred uses receive water before less preferred uses. Instead, some western states require **condemnation** and **compensation** in order to put a preference ranking to use. Other states use preference systems as they issue new water use permits, giving preference to higher-ranking water uses.

PRIORITY. The central feature of western water rights is the concept of priority. Whoever established a water use first in time has the higher-priority water right. Thus senior water rights holders occupy positions of superiority in relation to individuals whose rights are said to be junior.

The date a water user first appropriates water is the standard by which the right is ranked. A priority date is determined based on the water user's intent to appropriate (as was described earlier) and established in an administrative permit or a water decree granted by a court of law.

Priority takes on particular importance during times of water shortages. If

"Edgar rubs out the clothes." Montana Historical Society, Helena.

there is not enough water for both senior and junior appropriators, the prior appropriation doctrine allows the senior user to exercise his/her *full* water right before juniors receive any water. Junior rights thereafter are limited according to who is most junior in the priority ranking.

QUALIFICATIONS. Senior water rights are subject to some significant qualifications. A senior's use of water, for example, must ensure that stream conditions are not altered from those that existed at the time of a junior's priority date. Thus, senior users may not transfer their right to another party or change the place, purpose, or time of use if such alterations will harm a junior water user. Other qualifications may be set up in states that are becoming more strict in enforcing regulations that prohibit wasteful, polluting, and/or inefficient water use—for example, California, Arizona, and Washington.

ENFORCEMENT OF
PRIORITIES. Senior water rights
holders can **enforce** their claims
against junior water **appropriators** in
order to prevent interference with their
own beneficial water use by making a
call on the river. This may be accomplished by a personal visit with junior
users or may require the involvement
of the state engineer, a local water
commissioner, or the appropriate state
agency. However, a senior can't enforce
a water right if the junior user can
prove that the senior's use will not be
beneficial or if no water would reach
the senior (futile call).

What Waters May Be Appropriated?

Not all types of water may be appropriated for private use. Some state
constitutions define waters subject to
appropriation so that certain waters,
such as runoff and seasonal floods, are
excluded from private appropriation.

Do Limits Exist to Appropriation Rights?

In principle, the amount of water to
which a water user is entitled is limited to that used continuously and
beneficially from the time of first use.
However, in many states, old notices of
appropriation and permits often exag-
gerated the actual amounts of water
diverted and needed. Today, such over-
statement is increasingly rare, because
states now rely on verification by professional engineers before new water
rights are granted.

Other limitations come from historical
court cases where upstream miners were
prevented from polluting water to avoid
harming downstream users. In spite of
such judicial precedents, water quality
standards have not commonly been used
to limit continued beneficial use.

The Public Trust Doctrine

The Public Trust Doctrine potentially
casts a far-reaching shadow over existing water rights. A 1983 landmark ruling of the California Supreme Court
(commonly called the Mono Lake decision) held that under the Public Trust
Doctrine, long-standing water rights
could be reconsidered, and possibly
curtailed, if necessary to protect the
public interest.[9]

The Mono Lake decision put the city of
Los Angeles on notice that a challenge
launched by the National Audubon
Society could proceed. The decision
prompted many factual determinations.
It led to a Memorandum of
Understanding between the Los
Angeles Department of Water and
Power and the Mono Lake Committee
establishing a plan whereby the city
would use reclaimed wastewater (up
to thirty-five thousand acre-feet) to
replace water it has historically
diverted from the Mono Lake basin.

Although the Mono Lake decision is fairly recent, the Public Trust Doctrine dates to ancient Roman civil law and more recently to English common law. In the view of noted legal scholar Harrison Dunning, the decision validates that the ancient public trust doctrine may in the proper circumstances serve to limit how much water may be diverted pursuant to an appropriative right.[10]

The Mono Lake decision was made in California—to resolve a specific water use conflict. It has direct bearing only on the conditions of that case. Some observers have applauded it (and other public trust decisions) for attempting to redress a perceived imbalance between historical consumptive water use and more recently valued environmental (and non-consumptive) uses. Others view such applications of the public trust as an unjustified intrusion into the prior appropriation system that already provides protection for public trust uses.

Regardless of the interpretation of the Mono Lake decision, western states have continued to apply the Public Trust Doctrine in varying ways and to different case-specific circumstances and may continue to do so. Needless to say, the Mono Lake decision and the Public Trust Doctrine itself have generated much discussion and considerable controversy. The implications of the Public Trust Doctrine are cause for serious concerns among existing water rights holders. For those who favor nonconsumptive uses (e.g., fish and wildlife habitat), which lack legal standing under existing prior appropriation systems, the public trust offers them hope. How and whether the doctrine will be applied further in the West remains to be seen.

How Are Water Rights Obtained?

When the prior appropriation system first emerged, there was no central governmental authority or any systematic method for keeping records. When conflicts arose between water users, they were settled in court—or fistfights!

But the "lawsuit system" for clarifying water rights was slow, expensive, and inefficient. California was the first to create laws to establish a more uniform and efficient water appropriation system. The state did this in 1873 by writing local custom into law. Montana was the last western state to follow suit. It trailed a full century behind California, using a form of "lawsuit system" until 1973.[11]

California's water laws require:

- posting notice of quantity, purpose, and place of use of water at the diversion point;

- recording the use in the county records within ten days; and

- completing the appropriation and applying it to a beneficial use with due diligence.

"PRE-PERMIT" WATER RIGHTS. Across the West, many water rights (and in some states, claims) predate permit systems that were established later. These pre-permit rights are recognized as perfected rights. In most states, perfected water rights are considered to be appurtenant to the land. They are commonly acquired when land is conveyed, by deed or contract, to a new owner. In some states, such l ong-standing water rights may also be purchased outright, having been detached (or **severed**) from the land.

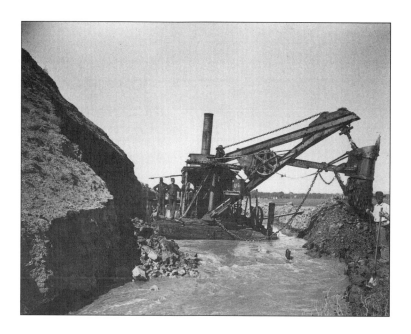

"Dredge at work on Carbon Hill, enlarging ditch." 1896.
Montana Historical Society, Helena.

One water diversion technique in California.

PERMIT SYSTEMS. The first permit system was adopted by Wyoming in 1890. Today, all western states have legal systems to allocate water rights and to administer water use. Most states have located this authority in an administrative agency. Only Colorado has vested this responsibility in the judicial system. (See the Colorado profile in Part IV.)

The purpose of western states' permitting procedures is twofold:

• to provide an orderly means of appropriating water

• to provide an orderly means of regulating established water rights.

The permitting systems of most states provide for the approval of a permit application if the applicant follows proper state procedures. In addition, the decision-making authority (e.g., the state engineer) must also find that unappropriated water is available and that a new water use will not harm the public welfare.

PERMIT PROCEDURES. The first step in obtaining a new water use permit is to file a formal application with the state engineer or administrative body (e.g., Department of Natural Resources, Water Resources Control Board). Commonly, this step should be completed before any physical work, such as digging a canal, is begun. If all permit requirements are met, the date of filing becomes the water right's priority date.

Public notice of a water use permit application is the next procedural step. This usually involves placing a notice in an appropriate newspaper and directly notifying all others who might be affected by a new water use permit. An objection period is then defined to allow others an opportunity to voice any concerns. Next, the decision-making entity must conduct a public hearing at which the permit applicant and any objectors are heard. At that time, the factual evidence is presented. Then the decision maker approves or disapproves the permit application, sometimes with modifications.

The permit decision rests on whether the evidence presented satisfies the state's required permit criteria. Montana's example is fairly representative. For a Montana permit, evidence must prove

• a beneficial use

• availability of unappropriated water at the time and period of use

• no harm to prior appropriators

• adequate diversion facilities

• no interference with reservations of water for future or planned uses

A Representative Example of State Water Permit Requirements—Montana

A new water use permit in Montana requires the following data:

1. Name of claimant and watercourse

2. Quantity of water

3. Time of use

4. Legal description of point of diversion

5. Purpose of use

6. Date of application to beneficial use

7. Other supportive evidence, such as a map or aerial photograph

If an application is approved, a permit is issued. Initially, this permit is not a water right. If all conditions of the permit are met within a specified time period (e.g., diversion structures are built and the water is put to beneficial use), then the water right is said to vest. At that time, the permit acquires a priority date fixed as the date the application was filed.

Many state administrative authorities put conditions on new water permits that describe how a water right is to be used. Some states also issue temporary and seasonal water use permits. For example, California issues such permits if unappropriated waters are determined to be available and if downstream water users and the environment are not harmed.

States may also reject water use permit applications on the grounds that they are not in the public interest. The states of Alaska, Utah, New Mexico, Washington, Idaho, and California are among those that have applied public interest criteria to reject new water use permits.

State administrative agencies generally regulate water allocations by enforcing established rights. Thus, water use by individuals and groups is subject to regulatory and administrative controls.

Alaska's Public Interest Criteria

1. Benefit to the water use permit applicant

2. Effect of resulting economic activity

3. Effect on fish and game and recreation

4. Public health effects

5. Possible loss of future alternative uses

6. Harm to others

7. Intent and ability of applicant

8. Effect on access to navigable or public waters

May a Water Right Be Transferred?

Most water rights can be transferred by sale, lease, or exchange in all appropriation states. Each state has its own laws and regulations that establish procedures for accomplishing water rights transfers within state boundaries.

Transfers can occur when the sale of land includes water rights put to use on that land. Other specific restrictions may come into play if land transfers also involve a change of water use to different locations, for different purposes, at different times, or to a new diversion point.

In most western states, perfected water rights pass with a land sale unless the transaction specifies otherwise. If land is divided at sale, then a portion of a water right attached to that land may accompany each subdivision.

In some states, water rights may be separated (or severed) from land when it is passed to another owner. Some states have defined restrictions if such transfers involve water uses away from the land: Montana, Oklahoma, Nebraska, Nevada, South Dakota, and Wyoming. Portions of water rights can also be sold, irrespective of land transactions, in some states. Water rights can also be made nonseverable by state law. Finally, conditions can be attached to severances to protect other users.

May a Water Right Be Changed?

If water users decide to change the way they use their water rights, they must apply to the appropriate state administrative agency or court for approval to do so. (Appropriate state agency contacts are listed with each state profile in Part IV.)

Water rights changes can include any of the following:

- a change in the point of diversion (or point of return)

- a change in the place of water use

- a change in the purpose of water use

- a change in the time of water use

States oversee water rights changes to ensure that alterations in water use do not harm other water users. A change in the point of diversion or return could decrease the amount of water a neighbor is entitled to by eliminating return flows. If the place of water use is changed, the needs of different soils might require more water and have the potential to harm others. A change in the purpose of use usually means from irrigation to municipal or industrial uses. These must also be considered to avoid subsequent harm to others.

"Steamer 'Helena' at Wolf Point, Missouri River," Summer 1880.
Haynes Foundation Collection, Montana Historical Society, Helena.

Even junior water rights holders are protected from harm from water rights changes sought by seniors.[12] In most states, the person seeking the change bears the burden of proving that no harm will result.

Public interest considerations can also play a role in denying a water right change. In applying public interest criteria, the environmental, economic, or social effects may be considered. Sometimes changes are approved conditionally, with specific requirements (or conditions) imposed to protect others from harmful environmental, economic, or social effects.

Can a Water Right Be Lost?

Water rights obtained under the prior appropriation system can be lost if they are not put to use. Most states define nonuse in relation to a defined period of time and require that intent be established before a right is considered abandoned. In some states, water rights may be forfeited for nonuse in spite of a water user's intent otherwise. In cases of forfeiture, all or a portion of a water right may be lost involuntarily because it has not been used for a period of time established in state law. Once a water right is formally determined to have been abandoned or forfeited, that water is available for appropriation by others or goes to satisfy subsequent rights. Beyond abandonment and forfeiture, there may be instances in which water rights are condemned by the state or federal government, for example, to establish a right-of-way (**eminent domain**). When a condemnation occurs, the original owner of the right must receive just compensation.

How Are Conflicts among Water Users Resolved?

Individuals or groups who possess water rights may sue others for violations of their rights. Court decisions that result from such lawsuits bind only the parties to the lawsuit. Some western states give administrative bodies the authority to resolve water disputes. Where this is true, the decision of that authority is subject to judicial review.

Other western states are now exploring ways to solve water resource disputes without litigation. Mediation, informal discussions facilitated by a neutral third party, and informal hearings between those in conflict are techniques currently in use in the West.

Are State Agency Water Rights Decisions Final?

A water rights decision made by an appropriate state administrative official or judicial agency is considered final unless it is appealed to a higher authority or a court of law within prescribed time limits.

What Are Federal and Tribal Reserved Water Rights?

The doctrine of reserved water rights evolved to ensure that Indian reservations and public lands set aside by the federal government would have sufficient water to fulfill the purposes for which they were established. Whereas most western water rights (so-called state-based appropriative rights) have a priority date based on when water was first put to beneficial use, federal reserved water rights have a priority date that goes back at least as far as the date on which the lands were set aside.

The reserved water rights doctrine is rooted in a number of judicial decisions, beginning with a U.S. Supreme Court decision that has come to be called the Winters Doctrine. The case of *Winters v. United States* involved a dispute between Native Americans of the Ft. Belknap Reservation and non-native settlers over the use of the Milk River in Montana. When the water use of the settlers upstream from the reservation interfered with the Indians' water need for large irrigation diversions, the U.S. government filed a lawsuit on the reservation's behalf.

The *Winters* decision held that when Congress created the Ft. Belknap Reservation, sufficient water to make the Indians a "pastoral and civilized people" was implicitly set aside. Therefore, although the nonnative settlers had perfected their water rights under Montana state law, the water right of the Indians of Ft. Belknap was prior.

The rationale used in the *Winters* decision on behalf of Native Americans also applies to public lands held by the federal government for national parks, wildlife refuges, national forests, military bases, wilderness areas, or other public purposes. It holds that when Congress authorized the establishment of federal land, it implicitly intended to reserve enough water to fulfill congressional purposes. Subsequent judicial decisions authorize federal reserved water rights on lands set aside by statute, treaty, or executive order. They are defined by the documents that set the land aside (treaty, executive order, statute) and recognized within individual states by negotiation or litigation.

Unlike state rights under prior appropriation systems, federal reserved water rights may remain unused for many years. This fact generates much concern on the part of state water administrators and water rights holders who fear that existing water allocation regimes will be disrupted once reserved rights are exercised. Regardless of the uncertainty such reserved rights create, states cannot prevent the eventual exercise of these federal property rights in water.

Federal reserved rights are limited to the purposes of the reservation of land and to quantities sufficient to fulfill these purposes. A federal case, *United States v. New Mexico*, ruled that when quantifying federal reserved rights, quantities are limited to the minimum amount necessary to fulfill the purposes for which the land was set aside.

Reserved water rights can be quantified in several ways. The most common method is adjudication. For Indian water rights, one mechanism is the practicably irrigable acreage (PIA) standard. Developed in another lawsuit (*Arizona v. California*), PIA is determined by examining soil characteristics, **hydrology**, engineering, and economics to determine the quantity of water associated with a federal reserved water right. Irrigable lands would also be identified, and the physical and financial feasibility of building water delivery systems would be established.

Another way to determine water quantities involved in a reserved water right is through a negotiated agreement. For example, Montana established a Reserved Water Rights Compact Commission to negotiate federal and tribal reserved water rights. Several compacts have been negotiated: with the Ft. Peck Reservation, with the Northern Cheyenne Reservation, and with the National Park Service for Glacier and Yellowstone National

Parks. The states of Colorado, Arizona, California, and Utah have also reached reserved water rights agreements through negotiation.

Once reserved water rights have been quantified, such rights may be used for purposes different from those for which they were quantified. For example, the Native American tribes along the Colorado River may choose to change the use of their reserved water right—which was quantified for agricultural use—to industrial use.

As a general rule, the federal government has given up control of privately held water rights to the states. However, the doctrine of intergovernmental immunity prevents states from regulating federal and tribal reserved water rights without consent or specific congressional mandate.

CHAPTER THREE:

WHAT'S THE PROSPECT FOR WESTERN WATER RIGHTS IN THE TWENTY-FIRST CENTURY?

Your grandfather might have been a good man and your father before you, but times now and then are different. It is the present to which you must adapt yourself.

—"Maxims for the Irrigated Farm"[13]

In the development of institutions there is always a conflict between custom and necessity. Through custom people cling to old traditions and try to perpetuate them by adapting them to new conditions, but necessity argues the case on its merit without much regard for precedent. Out of the conflict comes a compromise in which the old is modified and adapted.

—Walter Prescott Webb

The western water rights system of prior appropriation was developed to meet the needs of pioneer settlers and developers of the arid West. The system facilitated development of limited water supplies and to varying degrees controlled speculation. For example, the principles of priority and beneficial use ("use it or lose it") helped to protect the hard work and investments that were required to convert undeveloped land to productivity. These devices have served well.

Today, the West is settled. When we speak of converting undeveloped land to productivity, we are more likely to be thinking of constructing condominiums, a new ski area, or housing subdivisions than of the agricultural enterprises characteristic of yesteryear. How has the western water rights system weathered the changes of the last century? How will it adapt to conditions in the future?

Answers to the first question—How has the western water rights system weathered the changes of the last century?—vary dramatically. Many western landowners, particularly those who enjoy senior water rights, feel that the system "ain't broke, so there's no need to fix it." Other westerners, particularly wildlife biologists and recreationists who have seen streams go dry, have serious concerns about whether the water rights system is fair. After all, fish and wildlife and habitat

needs are late entrants into the "priority-based" water allocation regimes begun years ago.

These clashes are representative of the wide range of changing demands that are being placed on the West's limited water resources. Over the last twenty years, many states have taken steps to adapt their water law and water rights procedures to address emerging needs and new social priorities. Familiarity with some of these key concerns points the way to what may be priority western water rights issues in the future.

Reallocation of Water Resources

In the past, providing water for all who needed it was the primary concern. On the surface, things are not much different today. Tremendous amounts of time, energy, and dollars continue to be spent providing water for all who need it. Differences emerge, however, when one considers that when the West was being settled, most effort involved the allocation of water resources. Today a considerable percentage of the West's water has been allocated. In many cases, more water rights have been given out than there is water available to supply them!

In most western states, the challenge of meeting today's water needs has thus become a question of reallocating water resources. That is, how shall water be

"Fort Peck Dam Construction." June 24, 1937.
Montana Historical Society, Helena.

apportioned (and reapportioned) to support changing uses and different social priorities and to address newly perceived or future needs?

Several methods have evolved to address these questions. Water rights transfers, water rights changes, water marketing, water leasing, water salvage, instream flow protection, and temporary or conditional water use permits have all been used in western states. The state profiles that follow in Part IV describe some of these techniques in further detail.

Some of these methods are put in practice through states' water permitting processes. Water rights transfers, changes, and temporary or conditional use permits provide flexibility that allows for existing water rights holders to adapt their water uses. At the same time, because application for such changes is a prerequisite under most state laws, water managers remain informed about who is using what water, how much, and where.

Many western states also allow for water rights to be bought and sold separately from the land to which they have been attached. In some cases, such marketing is as simple a transaction as transferring a deed. In other states, water marketing is legally difficult and too politically hot to even touch.

One of the most troublesome issues in recent times has been ensuring sufficient stream flows to protect fish, wildlife, and riparian habitat. Most western states have developed methods to address these needs. Some states have written laws that provide specific authority to state agencies to apply for instream flow permits comparable to the traditional water right. Alaska even allows private individuals to seek such rights. At the other extreme, New Mexico has no formal legislated means to protect instream flows. However, this has not prohibited water users from working out streamflow management conditions to protect high-priority recreational needs.[14] This issue will likely persist well into the future.

The Endangered Species Act

The Endangered Species Act, passed by Congress in 1973 and substantially amended in 1982, can have significant consequences for existing water uses and water rights across the West. The act protects plant and animal species determined to be threatened with or in danger of extinction by prohibiting hunting, harassment, collection, or capture of identified species. Once a species has been listed, the responsible federal agency is then required by law to initiate programs to recover that species. The act also requires that all federal agencies ensure that their actions, including those on federal lands considered critical habitat, do not harm any plant or animal species listed as threatened or endangered.

One commonly asked question is: What about water rights necessary to protect endangered species? Although the Endangered Species Act does not create a water right, it does create an obligation. It requires that water management and allocation under existing water rights occur in a manner that does not violate provisions of the act. This responsibility can compel citizens and state and federal water managers to adapt their management practices.

The Endangered Species Act has been applied in numerous locations in the West. In relation to water resources, the act commonly applies when existing (or proposed) water uses could have a negative impact on critical habitat areas, as defined by the U.S. Fish and Wildlife Service (for terrestrial aquatic species) or the National Marine Fisheries Service (for marine animals and salmon).

The far-reaching effects of these applications of the act include alterations in existing water uses (e.g., reductions in reservoir releases from Glen Canyon Dam on the Colorado River), purchase and retirement of existing water rights (in the Upper Colorado River basin), and cessation of private pump irrigation when endangered species were consumed (e.g., the Glen-Calusa Irrigation District in California).

The real and potential ramifications of the Endangered Species Act for existing water rights are controversial and complex. As the act undergoes reauthorization, changes are likely to be made. At this writing, the Endangered Species Act stands firm. There has yet to be a single successful challenge to federal measures instituted to protect threatened and endangered species, including instances in which existing water rights (state appropriative *and* federal reserved) have been overridden by the far-reaching provisions of the act.

Conservation and Water Use Efficiency

In addition to the trend toward resource reallocation, a second trend that has emerged across the western United States is the growing importance of water **conservation** and water use efficiency. As populations increase, competition for water is forcing states and individuals to reevaluate water use practices and take steps to stretch the resource as far as possible. A number of states now require municipal water rights holders to institute conservation programs as a condition of their continuing and expanding water use. Other states prohibit water waste and go so far as to institute fines for violations. This trend is sure to persist.

Integrating the Management of Water Quality and Water Quantity

Water quality protection has become a high priority. Some parts of the West are working to redress the environmental degradation that resulted from large-scale mineral and resource extraction in the past. In other areas, the growth of subdivisions, industrial development, and dams has solved some problems (such as the need for affordable housing, jobs, water storage, and power production) only to create others (such as ground water pollution and overdraft, toxic waste disposal, and loss of salmon runs). Additionally, pollution from diffuse or **nonpoint sources**, such as stormwater runoff and agricultural land use, is receiving stronger emphasis and attention in federal and state laws and regulations.

"Opening of North Side Canal," March 23, 1908.
Idaho State Historical Society #P1984–101.6/a.

Unfortunately, most western states have traditionally divided the administrative protection of public health (water quality) from that of water allocation (water quantity). This has led to an unrealistic separation of two natural attributes that are integral to one another. Some states now recognize the false separation and are taking steps to combine or integrate their management of water quality and water quantity. Washington, for example, houses governmental authority for these concerns in a single Department of Ecology. Montana continues to have two different state management entities but is developing regulations that will make water quality a criterion for water use permit decisions.

Museum of North Idaho photo.

What's the Public Interest?

All western states deem water a public resource, so the public has a continuing interest in how water is used and allocated. But protecting a broad public interest can be a challenging task. Judicial decisions applying public trust obligations of state governments are one particularly significant example. Traditionally, the Public Trust Doctrine dealt with control of navigable waters to protect potential future public uses. More recently the doctrine has been used as the basis for reexamining established water rights in California, stream access in Montana, and other public interests in other states. Future applications of public trust obligations will likely vary state by state, if the doctrine is applied at all.

In addition to applications of the Public Trust Doctrine, many states have created special protective measures: special consideration for residents of **river basins** from which water is exported (**area of origin protection**), minimum stream-flow protection, and measures to evaluate the effects of water appropriations and transfers on the general welfare (public interest criteria). Where such measures are in place, they are described in the state profiles in Part IV.

The foregoing concerns and issues are frequently addressed through state water policies created by legislatures or through state regulations created to implement state and federal laws. As such, they may seem far removed from individual landowners and water users. But the increasing complexity of water issues shows that there is much to be gained by involving individual landowners and water users in water management decision-making in their "own backyards."

Watershed Management

Watershed management approaches, recommended early in our nation's history by John Wesley Powell, the visionary seer of western water, have renewed credibility. As a result, there is a trend toward greater involvement of water users from all sectors of society in the oversight and management of local water resources. This means that landowners, planners, government officials, and other citizens are being called upon to take more active and personal roles in their communities' management of scarce water resources. How this trend will work out and how it will relate to water rights and western water allocation remains to be seen. One positive potential, however, is that increased communication at the local level could help build bridges and develop positive relationships between those traditionally at loggerheads. In contrast, there may also be instances, such as disputes between states over water resources, where local-level watershed management solutions may be problematic.

Idaho State Historical Society #78-24.

Photo by: Mr. Ashizuka.

Interstate Water Allocation and Disputes

Increasing and changing demands for western water resources have led to disputes between states that have competing needs and claims to major river systems that cross states' boundaries. Such disputes are resolved in several ways. Interstate compacts, congressional action (legislation), and litigation have historically been the most commonly used techniques.

An **interstate compact** is a formal agreement approved by the participating states and Congress. It is the result of negotiation and congressional legislative approval of a final agreement arranged between states. Water compacts differ in their scope, structure, and achievements. They have been used to address navigation, fishing rights, boundary, water apportionment, pollution, water planning, and flood-control problems. Some interstate compacts declare policy or rights; others establish long-term administrative commissions.

A second means for resolving interstate water disputes is through congressional action. The U.S. Constitution gives Congress the authority to apportion interstate waters. Several judicial decisions challenging congressional action (for example, *Arizona v. California*) have affirmed and validated this responsibility.

Litigation between states over shared water resources occurs in the U.S. Supreme Court, which has original and exclusive jurisdiction. (If a person in one state sues another state or a person in another state, the U.S. District Court usually has jurisdiction.) In resolving disputes, the doctrine of equitable apportionment, which obliges states to share water resources, is the guiding principle. If a state's share of an interstate water resource is adversely affected by the actions of another state, the state whose interests have been violated may ask the U.S. Supreme Court to equitably apportion the water resource.

Interstate compacts, case law, and legislation have each been used to settle disputes. In 1982, for example, the U.S. Supreme Court ruled in *Sporhase v. Nebraska* that ground water is an article of commerce and that a Nebraska law restricting lawful water exports was unconstitutional. At the time of this writing, some other examples include an attempt to force reexamination of the basic interstate allocation of the Colorado River (the Colorado Compact), a struggle between the upper and lower basin states of the Missouri River basin over perceived inequities dating to original historical developments on the river, a dispute between Texas and New Mexico over interpretation of the Pecos River Decree, and a conflict between the upper and lower basins on the Platte River over the impacts of upstream development on downstream water uses.

Resolving interstate water disputes can be a slow process. One fact seems assured. Interstate water conflicts are likely to continue to occur in the future. The nature and shape of future solutions remain to unfold.

PART III
Cautions for
New and
Potential Landowners

Delighted with my new land purchase, I began excavation of a small hollow that promised to make a perfect pond for my children's recreation. After several weeks of hard work and considerable expense, I was ready to fill the pond by pumping water from the river that runs adjacent to my land. That was when the phone call from my neighbor revealed that I needed to have permission to use water from the river. More shocking, though, was his comment that I should have gotten state approval before I even built the pond —on my own property! After all my hard work and expense, I was ready for a fight. Was I surprised when my attorney informed me that my neighbor was right! I did need permission in order "to divert and impound water" on my own land! She advised me to stop my work and contact the Water Resource Department right away! Before long, I was sorry that I'd ever dug the pond, for I learned that the river running by my property is "fully appropriated." No new water diversions can be made from that source!

The foregoing situation may not have actually happened, but it is certainly not far-fetched in the arid western states. New and even longtime landowners have many tales to tell about the painful lessons they have learned about water rights. Perhaps such lessons might have been avoided had landowners been better informed about water rights and related rules and regulations.

In many parts of the West, informal means for allocating water have also been adopted by local water users. Such unwritten water use customs can be as important as water laws and rules for the new landowner to learn.

So, what does the discerning land-owner need to know about water rights? Familiarity with the information in the preceding chapters lays a good foundation of water rights knowledge. But what about some special assistance for the potential or new landowner who hopes to avoid water rights problems? What can the new landowner do to avoid such problems? What questions should be asked about water rights before purchasing land? Is there some type of "homework" that the landowner can do to learn more about his/her water right? And are there any responsibilities associated with owning a water right?

Answers to these and other questions are the focus of this section, which should help prepare the reader to become a more trouble-free holder of a water right.

TIP 1:

Before making a land purchase, consider whether you will need water. If so, what will you use it for?

CAUTION: Try to anticipate your water needs. Plan ahead!

TIP 2:

Contact the appropriate state water management agency (and your attorney) when selling or buying land to find answers to the following questions:

Does an existing water right remain with the land upon its sale? If so, is some type of official transfer (of the water right) required when a land purchase occurs? If a water right changes owners, must it be publicly recorded and advertised? How and where? Who is responsible for this?

Are there any restrictions regarding buying, selling, and moving a water right both geographically within a basin and also between different uses?

CAUTION: It's wise to take extra precautionary steps (beyond consultations with your realtor and title company) to learn about your state's laws regarding land sales and water rights.

TIP 3:

Obtain the assistance of appropriate and qualified professionals to help you learn more about water availability for your land.

For example, is it possible to acquire a new water right (surface or ground water) from potential sources of supply? Have previous water development activities been successful?

Attorneys, appropriate water managers, hydrologists, and hydrogeologists are all important resources to help you determine water availability for your land. It is rare to find one person who is qualified in both the legal and environmental aspects of such research.

CAUTION: Be suspicious of "off-the-cuff" assessments of your water right or water availability without documentation and/or evidence of historic water use and water rights.

TIP 4:

Investigate the water supply conditions (legal and physical) on or adjacent to the land.

For example, find out answers to the following questions:

• Is there a developed water source already on the land? (Examples include a domestic well, a pump at the river, an irrigation pump, irrigation canals, and a stock pond.)

• Is a water right associated with the development?

• Is water physically available?

• You might be able to conduct your own resource inventory. Do you see water in the stream or river near your property? Is tap water available on the property? Does the pump on the property work? Does it yield water adequate for your use?

TIP 5:

Some possible additional information sources to examine include: U.S. Geological Survey Stream Gauge records for surface water availability, well-log records available from appropriate water management agencies to determine ground water availability, published state and federal reports and investigations, and Water Resource Center libraries at land grant universities.

CAUTION: Never assume that water is automatically available for whatever use you desire simply because you see it physically present!

Do your homework: Investigate the formal and official water right record of the stream, watercourse, or ground water source!

First, determine what type of water right(s) presently exist in your area. To what limitations are they subject?

Second, examine the formal and official water right record of the neighboring stream or watercourse. The formal record often identifies the maximum limits of water use from a given water source. *(See your state's profile in Part IV for the agency you should contact.)*

When examining the record, try to determine the following:

• What are the maximum limits of use and the limits to the duty of water?

• Has the record been verified some how, as through a general stream adjudication, court decree, or court decision?

• If a general adjudication is occurring, what stage has the process reached? Has a claim been filed? How should you be involved?

• What is the status of an application or permit?

- Is there a physical record of the landowner's interest in an irrigation company or homeowner's association with water rights?

- Has the rural subdivision (particularly in desert regions) within which you are purchasing land complied with state laws and regulations to ensure that water supplies are adequate?

Third, ask what type of system exists for allocating water among users on the stream. For example, is water delivered strictly on the basis of priority date? Is a preference system used to divide water from the watercourse?

CAUTION: Because the formal and official record does not document customary day-to-day management of water in a given area, learn about customary (or informal) water use in your area.

TIP 6:

Investigate ditch or other conveyance easements associated with your property.

It is not uncommon for ditch rights or other conveyance facilities to be held separately from water rights.

CAUTION: Don't assume one type of property right transfer necessarily includes another.

TIP 7:

Investigate the informal record of water use.

If making a new land purchase, try to visit with present or previous landowners to learn the details and variations of local water use customs. Other important contacts to make are neighboring water users, ditch riders or water commissioners, irrigation companies or districts, homeowners' associations, and water management agency field staff.

The following are some good questions to ask:

- Has the water supply ever been limited or interrupted as the result of a call by a senior or other priority water user? If so, how frequently is call made? Every year? Midsummer? Late summer? Right after spring runoff?

- How is call made between water users on this source?

- Is a commissioner, ditch rider, or mayordomo appointed, formally or informally?

- What are local customs related to diversion and operation of diversion systems? (For example, who operates headgates? What notice is provided to other water users? Who maintains ditches? What type of formal or informal organization exists to deal with these issues locally?)

- What is the past owner's perception of physical availability, effects of localized drought, and changes in water availability due to changing land use activities that may affect water supply? (For example, have irrigation methods or patterns changed in the area? Has basin vegetative cover changed as a result of logging, mining, or housing developments?)

CAUTION: Taking the time to learn about local water use customs can pay dividends by helping you develop friendly and positive relationships with neighboring landowners!

TIP 8:

If you obtain your water from a private, quasi-public, or public vendor, such as an irrigation district, a rural water company, or a municipal water supply system, investigate the nature of their service.

In some cases, such services are for sale, and the vendor owns and controls the water right. However, some water user associations, ditch companies, and mutual irrigation companies may provide only a delivery service and the user must have a water right.

CAUTION: The old adage "Let the buyer beware" is good advice for the new landowner who relies on others for his or her household water supply.

TIP 9:

Your deed to your property and your water right are not the same thing.

CAUTION: Water rights are acquired from the state; land is transferred privately, from person to person.

TIP 10:

In many states, in order to develop water on another's land, permission or an easement must first be obtained.

For example, in the western states today, stock growers who hold federal grazing permits occasionally seek to develop water for their livestock's use. A grazing permit may not automatically entitle the holder to develop an associated water use.

CAUTION: If your proposed water development will encroach on another's land, be sure you have permission (or an easement) before beginning the development.

TIP 11:

Fully investigate the water right you are considering purchasing before you finalize the transaction.

Some water rights have not been used for so long that they may have been lost through nonuse or forfeited.

CAUTION: Don't assume a water right you are considering purchasing is valid. Check it out with your state water allocation agency first!

At this point the reader is prepared to avoid the situation described by common, old-time "ditch wisdom" in the West:

'Tis better to be upstream with a shovel and a shotgun than downstream with a priority date.

PART IV
Profiles of
Western States'
Water Rights
Systems

Lomen Brothers, photographers, PCA 28-93, Alaska State Library.

ALASKA

First Things First: What's the System?

Alaska is a prior appropriation state.[15] Some riparian uses of water were allowed early in the state's history, but when the Alaska Water Use Act was enacted in 1966, all riparian rights were converted to prior appropriation rights.

In Alaska, a water right is a legal authorization to use surface water or ground water. When a water right is acquired, it allows for the diversion, impoundment, or withdrawal of a specified quantity of water, from a specific source, for a specific use.

Landowners in Alaska don't have automatic rights to a ground water or surface water source. If, for example, a new landowner has a creek through her property, she must obtain a water right to protect her use. Simply using water doesn't give the landowner a legal right.

Who to Contact

The Division of Mining and Water Management of the Alaska Department of Natural Resources is the state government agency responsible for allocating surface water and ground water rights for all lands in Alaska, including private, municipal, state, and federal lands. Four regional offices are prepared to respond to public inquiries relating to water rights, water allocation, and water use.

Southcentral Region
3601 C Street, Suite 822
P.O. Box 107005
Anchorage, AK 99510-7005
(907) 269-8624

Northern Region
3700 Airport Way
Fairbanks, AK 99706-2703
(907) 451-2700

Southeast Region
400 Willoughby Avenue, 4th Floor
Juneau, AK 99801
(907) 465-3400

Mat-su/Copper Basin Area
1800 Glenn Highway, Suite 12
Palmer, AK 99645
(907) 745-7200

How to Get a Water Right in Alaska

The first step in obtaining a new water right in Alaska is for an individual to file an application with the Division of Mining and Water Management of the Department of Natural Resources. The proper application form must be accompanied by relevant documentation and a fee payment. The proposed application is reviewed, accepted, and indexed into a tracking system. Certain types of applications require public notice: those involving an appropriation of over five thousand gallons of water per day, those requiring water from an "anadromous" fish stream (one in which fish migrate upstream from the sea to breed), and those seeking water in a river or stream where there is a high level of competition. (The notice process includes certified mailings to prior appropriators who might be affected and to the Departments of Fish and Game and Environmental Conservation as well as legal notice in a local newspaper or post office. Each step provides for a fifteen-day comment period. Furthermore, all substantive objections must be addressed in writing before a permit can be issued.)

Once an application is processed, a permit is issued for a specific use (e.g., to drill a well or to divert water to a garden).

Sometimes a water permit contains specific conditions deemed necessary to protect prior appropriators and the public interest. Some examples are requiring that minimum flows be maintained for fish passage, that water use be metered and reported, and that plans of operation be submitted. After the water user establishes the full amount he/she will use and follows all conditions in the permit, a Certificate of Appropriation is issued, legally establishing the water right. The date an application is filed becomes the **priority date**.

The Division of Mining and Water Management applies four criteria when approving or rejecting an application:

- Will the rights of prior appropriators be unduly affected?

- Are the proposed means of diversion or construction adequate?

- Is the proposed use of water a beneficial use?[16]

- Is the proposed appropriation in the public interest?

Other Important Things to Know

In Alaska a water right attaches to the land where the water is being used for as long as the water is used. If the land is sold, the water right transfers to the new owner. The Division of Mining and Water Management has authority to approve severance of a water right from the land after public interest criteria have been considered.

Water for public water supplies may be granted as a preferred use in Alaska. This means that a prior water right is not absolute but may be subject to changes to meet public needs for domestic water use. If such changes need to be made, the prior water right holder must receive **just compensation** for his/her loss.

Abandonment and Forfeiture.

The state may declare an appropriation to be wholly or partially abandoned when a water right holder, with intent, abandons and fails to make use of all or part of his or her appropriation.

The state may declare an appropriation wholly or partially forfeited if an appropriator voluntarily fails or neglects, without sufficient cause, to make use of all or a part of his or her appropriated water for a period of five successive years.

The state of Alaska is unique in that it has legal authority to appropriate

Partridge, William H., PCA 88-55, Alaska State Library.

water to itself for purpose of sale. The water for sale must be deemed to be surplus to the needs within the hydrologic unit from which it is appropriated, an instream flow or level must be established, and a water conservation fee must be assessed.

Federal Lands in Alaska

Military Land	2.4 million acres
National Forests	23.2 million acres
BLM Reserved Land	26.1 million acres
National Parks	51 million acres
Fish & Wildlife Refuges	76 million acres

Adjudication and Federal Reserved Water Rights in Alaska

In 1986, the Alaska Water Use Act was amended to establish procedures for the Department of Natural Resources to conduct administrative basinwide adjudications clarifying the extent and nature of water rights. Federal reserved water rights are included if the federal government consents to have its federal reserved water rights administratively adjudicated by the state. Of the 367.7 million acres in Alaska, almost 49 percent, or more than 178 million acres, are federal lands, which may have federal reserved water rights.

Protecting Alaska's Public Water Resources in the Twenty-first Century

Water Planning and Management.

Alaska's water rights program is the cornerstone of the state's water resource management, because water is associated with every commercial, industrial, and domestic development in the state. Any use of a significant quantity of water requires a permit or certificate of appropriation.[17] The water rights program ensures that the use of water is in the public interest and in accordance with the state constitution. A Water Resources Board, appointed by the governor, helps to inform and advise the executive branch on all water matters, including prevention of pollution, water development, study of current water supplies, and planning for future water needs.

Instream Flow.

Private individuals, organizations, and government agencies may apply for reservations of water for instream use. Such rights may be granted to protect specific instream water uses, such as fish and their habitat, recreation, transportation, and water quality. Upon receiving an Application for Reservation of Water, the Division of Mining and Water Management must establish that there is a need for the reservation, that there will be no adverse impacts on other water right holders, and that the right is in the public interest. An assessment is also made to confirm that water is available for the reservation and that the information in the application is accurate and adequate.

An instream flow right in Alaska can be used to maintain a specified **flow rate** or level of water at a specific point or stream segment. The right may be year-round or seasonal. Such rights are subject to review every ten years. An instream flow reservation can keep later water users from appropriating water that may affect the instream activity. Unlike other water rights, instream reservation rights are optional.

Water Quality.

Water quality is a beneficial use in Alaska. It is also a criterion used to determine whether new water appropriations will be permitted. In addition, water quality can be a factor considered in reviewing applications for instream flow rights.

Public Interest Criteria.

Several public interest criteria are taken into consideration in water management decision-making in Alaska, as when new water uses are proposed. The public interest criteria considered include potential effects on resulting economic activity, fish and game resources, public recreation opportunities, and public health. Possible alternative uses of water and access to navigable or public waters are also taken into account.

For More Information

The Alaska Department of Natural Resources has more information about water rights in its *Water User's Handbook* and fact sheets. Copies of these publications and water rights applications are available at the regional office locations previously listed and at the Public Information Center.

Public Information Center
3601 C Street, Suite 200
P.O. Box 107005
Anchorage, AK 99503-5929
(907) 269-8400

ARIZONA

First Things First: What's the System?

Surface water and ground water rights are treated separately in Arizona. Rights to surface water are based on the prior appropriation doctrine. Allocation of rights to ground water varies depending on location.

Ground water **depletion** was recognized as a problem in Arizona in the early 1930s. Today the Ground Water Management Act requires rigorous conservation of ground water in Active Management Areas (AMAs) and Irrigation Non-Expansion Areas (INAs), where overpumping has been most severe. These particular areas underlie the major metropolitan areas and areas of intense agriculture.

To oversee ground water use and management, each AMA has a Ground Water Users Advisory Council, appointed by the governor. These groups develop water conservation plans to realize a goal of "safe yield." Safe yield occurs when the amount being pumped equals the amount of water recharged to the aquifer.[18]

Who to Contact

The Arizona Department of Water Resources is responsible for administering both the surface water and ground water codes that govern water uses in the state. Generally, the department controls who can use ground water, where it can be used, and how much can be withdrawn. In certain areas (such as AMAs or INAs), the department has extensive authority. In much of the state, however, the primary responsibility is record keeping.

Arizona Department of Water Resources
500 N. 3rd Street
Phoenix, AZ 85004-3903
(602) 417-2410

How to Get a Water Right in Arizona

A person wishing to use surface water in Arizona must file the proper application form with the Department of Water Resources. The application must describe the source of the water to be appropriated, the location of the proposed diversion (if any), the proposed place of use of the water, the proposed beneficial use, the quantity and periods of use, and any other information required. Filing is followed by review, public notice, and a protest period. If an application is protested, a public hearing may be held. Thereafter, the application may be granted if the proposed use (1) does not conflict with vested rights, (2) is not a menace to public safety, and (3) is not against the interests and welfare of the public.

Payment of a fee is required before the Department of Water Resources issues a permit, which generally allows five years for completion of the proposed water project. When the water has been put to use, a Certificate of Water Right is issued. However, even after receipt of a certificate, the surface water user is subject to review by the Arizona General Stream Adjudication. (See "Adjudication and Federal Reserved Water Rights.")

Individuals seeking to acquire a ground water permit also must file an application with the Department of Water Resources and pay a fee. As with surface water rights applications, once the application is determined to be complete and correct, public notice must follow. A protest period is allowed, and if an application is protested, a public hearing may be held. If a ground water permit is granted, the applicant will be entitled to a specific amount of water, withdrawn in a specific location for a specific purpose. The permit will be of limited duration, but the applicant may seek renewal.

Other Important Things to Know

In Arizona, surface water rights are considered to be attached to the land, so they may not be transferred at will. Rather, an application must be filed with the Department of Water Resources if one seeks to sever the water right from the land and transfer its use to a new location. If a water right has been used for domestic, municipal, or irrigation purposes, a right holder must also seek approval before changing the use of the water.

If a water right isn't used in Arizona for a period of five consecutive years, it may be deemed to have been forfeited. A water right holder may also voluntarily abandon the right. If a right is abandoned or forfeited, it reverts to the public, and that water becomes available for new appropriation.

Adjudication and Federal Reserved Water Rights

General stream adjudications are under way in the Gila and the Little Colorado river systems in Arizona. These judicial proceedings will determine the extent and priority of water rights in each basin. One goal of the adjudications is to integrate federal reserved rights into the state system of allocation. Another goal is to assess all uses in priority and quantity for improved water management ability.

The adjudications will take many years, because more than twenty-seven thousand people have filed more than seventy-seven thousand water rights claims. The Arizona Superior Court will eventually issue comprehensive final decrees defining water rights for the Gila and Little Colorado Rivers. Directly or indirectly, most Arizona residents will be affected by the adjudication procedures.

Native American water settlements are being integrated into the adjudication. Three water settlements (Salt River–Pima Maricopa Indian Community, Fort McDowell Indian Community, and Yavapai-Prescott Indian Tribe) have been accepted by the Adjudication Court and will be part of the final decree. The settlements provide a specific quantity of water to the tribe from a variety of sources. All water provided to the tribe is from voluntary participants in the settlement.

For more information about the general stream adjudication in Arizona, contact:

Office of the Special Master
Arizona General Stream Adjudication
Arizona State Courts Building
1501 W. Washington, Suite 228
Phoenix, AZ 85007
(602) 542-9600
FAX: (602) 542-9602

Protecting Arizona's Public Water Resources in the Twenty-first Century

Water Planning and Management. A critical function of the Arizona Water Resources Department is to serve as the repository of a vast amount of hydrologic and water use data for both surface water and ground water resources. As a result of the ongoing adjudication processes, water claims and water resources in each basin are described and inventoried. All wells in the state are recorded. The department tracks irrigated acreage within the AMAs through remote sensing and field checks to ensure that irrigation occurs only where permitted. Ground water levels are also monitored and mapped. In an arid state like Arizona, this information is critical to managing water resources for the present and future.

Arizona is one of the fastest-growing states in the West. Private development is very dependent on adequate water resources. Competing for water are nineteen Arizona Native American tribes and traditional agricultural and mining uses on federal and state-owned land. Ever-increasing visitation to national and state parks and recreation areas will also have an impact on Arizona's future water management.

Conservation and Prevention of Waste.

The Arizona Ground Water Management Code was developed to realize the goals of conservation and prevention of water waste. To reach safe-yield goals for ground water by 2025, conservation and prevention of waste are an absolute necessity in AMAs. The Ground Water Users Advisory Council in each AMA defines the methods that will be used to accomplish the goals.

Instream Flow.

Arizona recognizes stream-flow maintenance to support fish and wildlife as a beneficial use. Five instream flow permits have been issued. One of these has been fully developed, or certified, by the Department of Water Resources.

CALIFORNIA

First Things First: What's the System?

California's water appropriation system has been described as a plural system. This is because the state recognizes both the riparian and appropriation systems but also uses other legal doctrines to support rights, including those for ground water use.

Ground Water Rights. Three

legal classifications are recognized in California: "subterranean streams," "underflow of surface streams," and **percolating ground water**. Subterranean streams and underflow are subject to the law of surface waters and require a permit from the State Water Board for use. A permit is not required to use percolating ground water.

Riparian Rights. Landowners

whose property borders a stream, lake, or pond in California may enjoy riparian water rights that are incidental to their piece of land. Such rights are senior to most appropriative rights and may be used for beneficial purposes on riparian land without a permit. Several attributes of riparian rights have been defined, so landowners are advised to consult with the State Water Resources Control Board before diverting water adjacent to their land.

Appropriative Rights. Before

1872, a water right could be acquired in California merely by diverting and using water. In 1872, the state legislature created an alternative method: posting a notice of appropriation at the proposed point of diversion and recording a copy of the notice with a nearby county recorder. Both of these procedures were in effect until December 19, 1914. Since then, new appropriative water rights can be initiated only by applying to the State Water Board. Once a right is obtained, it must be maintained by continuous beneficial use. Both pre- and post-1914 appropriative rights can be lost by five or more continuous years of nonuse or by abandonment.

Who to Contact

The California State Water Resources Control Board (often called the State Water Board) is responsible for issuing water use permits and licenses for surface water and underground streams. The use of percolating ground water, riparian use of surface waters, and appropriative use of surface water begun before December 19, 1914, are under the authority of the California court system. However, state law requires riparian and pre-1914 diverters to file statements of water diversion and use with the State Water Board.

Water Resources Control Board
The Paul R. Bonderson Building
901 P Street
Sacramento, CA 95814
(916) 657-1359

How to Get a Water Right in California

California landowners seeking a new appropriation of water must file an application for a water right permit with the State Water Board. (New, small domestic water users must file a registration with the board.)

An application for a new water appropriation is approved if it is determined to be for a useful or beneficial purpose and unappropriated water is available. In making its decision, the board considers the relative benefits derived from all beneficial uses, possible water pollution, and water quality. All permits issued are subject to conditions.

Other Important Things to Know

Persons holding appropriative water rights in California may change the point of diversion, place of use, or purpose of use as long as others are not injured by such changes. Procedures also exist to transfer rights, temporarily or permanently. For example, the state allows for the sale, lease, or exchange of water rights, if such changes will not harm any legal user of water or cause unreasonable effects on fish, wildlife, or other instream beneficial uses. If an appropriative water right is not used in California for five years, the right to the water's use may revert to the public. Such a reversion, however, occurs only after notice is given and a public hearing is held. Water saved through conservation efforts, which is then used or reclaimed, is not subject to forfeiture.

Adjudication and Federal Reserved Water Rights

In California, adjudication of water rights can involve two procedures. One is initiated when a lawsuit relating to water rights is filed in court. In some cases, the court may ask the State Water Board to act as referee and to investigate and report.

A second adjudication procedure was established in the California Water Code. This statutory procedure can be used to determine all rights to the waters of any stream, lake, or other body of water (including percolating ground water under certain conditions). Such statutory adjudication is initiated when one or more persons claiming a right from a particular source files a petition with the State Water Board. The board then must decide if public interest and need require that adjudication occur. A decree that integrates all rights is the final result of such statutory adjudication.

Protecting California's Public Water Resources in the Twenty-First Century

Water Planning and Management. Several government agencies share responsibility for water management in California. The five-member Water Resources Control Board is appointed by the governor and

is responsible for the water rights and water quality functions of the state. The State Water Board has the authority to declare watercourses fully appropriated and has done so in specific cases.

California law also created the Department of Water Resources, which is responsible for planning for the use of state water supplies. A California Water Commission is also appointed by the governor and confirmed by the state senate. This body develops rules and regulations in consultation with the director of the Water Resources Department. Meetings of the commission are a useful forum for discussion of California water issues.

Conservation and Prevention of Waste. The prevention of water waste and unreasonable use are important components of California water law and policy, primarily to make more water available. Towns and cities may even be required to conserve and reclaim water as a condition of use.

Conservation goals were instituted when the state constitution was amended in 1928 to require reasonable diversion and use in the exercise of all water rights. The State Water Board and the courts share responsibility for applying and enforcing this requirement.

Instream Flow. California state
law and judicial decisions require
instream flow protection for fish and
wildlife. In practice, when a new water
use permit is sought, the State Water
Board must notify the Department of
Game and Fish, which may recommend
amounts of water necessary in the
affected stream to preserve fish,
wildlife, and recreation. The board then
considers these recommendations and
may set stream-flow requirements
accordingly.

COLORADO

First Things First: What's the System?

The prior appropriation doctrine is the basis of Colorado water law. Surface water rights are appropriated in order of priority. Prior appropriation of ground water also occurs, except as "modified to permit the full economic development of designated ground water resources" in designated ground water basins. Full expression of the state's water law is found in the state constitution, state statutes, and numerous court decisions.[19]

Who to Contact

Seven district courts (water courts) are responsible for issuing water rights in Colorado. The state engineer administers and distributes water and issues and denies permits to construct wells. However, a ground water right can only be obtained through formal application to a water court. The water court, in turn, cannot grant a ground water right until the state engineer issues a well permit.

Skinny dipping, South Canal.
Colorado Historical Society.

A Ground Water Commission with twelve members is responsible for designated basins in the eastern plains of Colorado. The commission's duties include administration of ground water rights, water conservation, and protection of vested water rights. The commission is also charged with establishing pumping levels in designated districts that will not deplete ground water supplies at a rate materially in excess of the reasonably anticipated average rate of future recharge.

The Colorado Water Conservation Board oversees conservation in the state and is responsible for protecting the natural flows and water levels in streams and lakes.

Division of Water Resources
1313 Sherman Street, Room 818
Denver, CO 80203
(303) 866-3581

How to Get a Water Right in Colorado

A ground water or surface water right is obtained in Colorado by filing an application in one of seven water courts in the state. Geographically located within major river basins, each court has an appointed water judge and water referee who consider all matters in their division.

Once a water right application is filed with the court, the application or a summary of it is published in "the resume," a monthly record of all applications filed with that division of the court. Publication is considered "notice" to all existing water owners that a new application for water is sought that could potentially affect other water rights. A sixty-day period follows, providing time for opposition statements to be filed with the court. Next, a water referee becomes fully informed about the application, its validity, and statements of opposition and then consults with a division engineer. Within thirty days, the engineer files a report summarizing the consultation. This is sent to the applicant, who must circulate copies of the report to all other parties in the case.

A referee's ruling can approve or disapprove a portion of an application or the entire request. The ruling may be protested by filing an outline of reasons for disagreement with the court.

A hearing is then conducted by a water judge. If no protest is filed, the referee's ruling is signed by the water judge and entered as a decree.

Decreed water rights are considered property rights in Colorado. As such, they can be bought, sold, and leased to others by conveyance of deed. The location and type of use may also be changed through the water court by providing evidence that such changes will not harm others' water rights. Terms and conditions may be attached to such changes.

Surface water and ground water rights in Colorado may be absolute or conditional. An absolute water right is one in which water has been diverted and put to a beneficial use. A conditional right provides the holder a right to develop water in the future while maintaining its priority date until the proposed development is complete. To maintain a conditional right, the holder must file an application for a finding of reasonable diligence or prove that completion of the project is being diligently pursued. At completion of the project, the holder of the conditional permit may file for an absolute water right.

Other Important Things to Know

Beneficial Use. This is defined in Colorado law as "the use of that amount of water that is reasonable and appropriate under reasonably efficient practices to accomplish without waste the purpose for which the appropriation is lawfully made." Impoundment of water for recreation, fish, and wildlife is a beneficial use. Minimum stream-flow purposes have also been deemed to be beneficial uses by the Water Conservation Board.

Abandonment and Forfeiture. A conditional water right may be deemed to have been abandoned if the holder of the right fails to file a statement proving reasonable diligence to complete the project. Ten years of nonuse of an absolute right is a presumption of abandonment; however, water rights cannot be forfeited in Colorado without proof of intent.

Adjudication and Federal Reserved Water Rights

Water rights are adjudicated by district water courts in Colorado.

Protecting Colorado's Public Water Resources in the Twenty-first Century

Water Planning and Management.

In an effort to achieve more efficient management of Colorado's water resources, state law requires the collection and study of data for both surface water and ground water supplies. The Ground Water Commission designates ground water basins and develops information on quantity of water stored, estimated use, and annual rate of discharge. Depletion rates are set for ground water in all parts of the state.

All declared surface water and ground water rights are published, in order of seniority.

Conservation and Prevention of Waste.

Both conservation and prevention of waste are important components of Colorado water law and water management. For example, ground water is "devoted to beneficial use in amounts based upon conservation of the resource and protection of vested water rights." Beneficial use is defined to explicitly exclude waste. Ground water resources are to be developed "consistent with conservation." The state engineer is required to prevent waste. Ditch owners are expected to keep their ditches in good repair to prevent waste. Even a State Projects Water Conservation Landscaping Act requires all public projects and facilities to conserve water by developing a landscaping plan to minimize water use.

Instream Flow.

Protection of instream flow is the exclusive responsibility of the Colorado Water Conservation Board. It has the authority to appropriate waters from streams and lakes "to preserve the natural environment to a reasonable degree." The board may acquire water as it deems necessary for minimum stream flows or for natural levels and volumes in lakes. It requests information to assist with its decision-making processes from the Colorado Department of Natural Resources' Divisions of Water, Outdoor Recreation and Wildlife, and the federal Departments of Agriculture and Interior.

IDAHO

First Things First: What's the System?

Prior appropriation is the basis for water appropriation in Idaho.

Who to Contact

The Idaho Department of Water Resources is responsible for the allocation of surface water and ground water. State law establishes the director of the department as the official responsible for water allocation, oversight of water distribution to those having rights, assistance to courts with the adjudication of water rights, processing of applications to change existing water uses, and enforcement of the water appropriation laws of the state. An eight-member Idaho Water Resource Board, appointed by the governor and approved by the state senate, provides guidance to the department and administers some water programs.

For information about water rights in Idaho, contact the nearest office of the Idaho Department of Water Resources or call toll-free 1-800-451-4129.

Western Region Office
2735 Airport Way
Boise, ID 83705
(208) 334-2190

Eastern Region Office
900 North Skyline
Idaho Falls, ID 83402
(208) 525-7161

Southern Region Office
222 Shoshone Street East
Twin Falls, ID 83301
(208) 736-3033

Northern Region Office
1910 Northwest Blvd. #210
Coeur d'Alene, ID 83814
(808) 856-4639

State Office
1301 N. Orchard Street
Boise, ID 83720
(208) 327-7900

How to Get a Water Right in Idaho

All new water rights (except small domestic ground water uses and instream stock water) are obtained by filing an application with the Idaho Department of Water Resources. Upon receipt of the application and payment of the filing fee, the department establishes the priority date for the proposed water use. This is followed by public notice of the new application for two consecutive weeks in a local county newspaper.[20] Protests may be filed by water users or any entity concerned about the application. An effort is made to informally resolve any concerns, and a hearing may be conducted to establish the record upon which the disputed issues are decided.

Several criteria are considered when evaluating an application for a new water right:

• The new use will not reduce the quantity of water available under existing water rights.

• The water supply is sufficient for the purposes of the new use.

• The application is made in good faith and not for speculation or delay.

• The applicant has sufficient financial resources to complete the project.

• The new use will not conflict with the "local public interest."[21]

• The project is consistent with the conservation of water in Idaho.

Final decision-making authority rests with the director of the Idaho Department of Water Resources. Those dissatisfied with the outcome may appeal to state district court.

Once approved, applications to appropriate water are called permits. The permit holder is given a specified period of time, but not more than five years, to prove that the water has been put to beneficial use. When beneficial

use is established and a fee is paid, a field examination is conducted. Finally, a license is issued confirming the water right.

Other Important Things to Know

A portion of the waters of the Snake River Basin is held in trust by the state of Idaho. Allocation of this water occurs similarly to the procedure described above, with consideration of additional criteria. First, the director must decide whether a proposed new water use will significantly reduce water flows available for power generation. If the answer is positive, further criteria are then applied.

When a water license is issued by the state, it is considered to be attached to the land upon which the right is used.

Water rights can be lost by abandonment or forfeiture. After five consecutive years of nonuse, a right may be considered to have been forfeited and open to new appropriation. Abandonment requires proof of intent.

If a water right holder wants to change the place, period, or nature of use or the point of a water diversion, an application to do so must be filed with the Department of Water Resources. Four criteria are applied by the department in its decision-making process:

• Will other rights, junior or senior, be injured by the change?

• Will the change cause an expansion in use of the right?

• Is the change in the local public interest?

• Will the change conserve water?

One year is granted to allow time for approved changes. The state has established **water bank** and rental pools to help facilitate temporary use of certain water rights.

An *Idaho Water Law Handbook* is available from the nearest office of the Idaho Department of Water Resources for $25.

Adjudication and Federal Reserved Water Rights

The state district court is responsible for the general adjudication procedure occurring in Idaho. Although rights to many of the streams and rivers of Idaho were determined by court actions years ago, the general adjudication of all rights in each drainage basin has yet to be accomplished. The task is a significant one. Until 1971 for surface water and 1963 for ground water, rights could be established by diversion and beneficial use without first acquiring a permit. Consequently, many unrecorded rights must be judicially validated.

The Snake River Basin Adjudication began in 1987. Its purpose is to identify and make a complete and accurate record of all water rights in the Snake River Basin and its tributaries and **drainage basins**. Geographically, the process involves thirty-eight of forty-four counties in the state and both surface water and ground water. This adjudication will allow the state to learn for the first time how much water is required to supply all persons identified as having water rights.

Although the adjudication process is a judicial proceeding, it involves the Idaho Department of Water Resources, which reviews each water right claim for accuracy. The director of the department then reports findings and makes recommendations to the court. Objections are heard, a hearing is held, and then a judgment is made. The final step is the issuance of a decree, which identifies each water right.

The result of the Snake River Adjudication will be better administration and delivery of water in times of shortage. It will also facilitate state efforts to plan water use and management more effectively in the future. When completed, the adjudication will result in technically correct and legally sufficient determination of all water rights for all water uses in the basin. Federal reserved water rights are also included in the process.[22]

To obtain a free copy of the *Snake River Basin Adjudication Water User's Handbook*, contact the nearest office of the Idaho Department of Water Resources.

Protecting Idaho's Public Water Resources in the Twenty-first Century

Conservation and Prevention of Waste.
Conservation and prevention of waste may be employed as conditions on water rights permits issued by the Idaho Department of Water Resources.

Instream Flow.
Water appropriation rules include a number of criteria for promoting instream flows. One is the possible effects of a new water diversion on fish and wildlife habitat and water quality. Additionally, public agencies have the authority to request the right to maintain minimum stream flows from the Water Resource Board. Water rights permits may also include conditions that protect established minimum stream flows.

Water Quality.
Quality standards may also be applied as conditions on water rights permits to ensure compliance.

Public Interest Criteria.
These criteria are applied in the review of applications for new water rights. Public interest criteria also influence allocation of water made newly available from earlier appropriation to hydropower production.

KANSAS

First Things First: What's the System?

Kansas has a prior appropriation system governed by a statutory permit procedure, applying to both surface water and ground water.

Who to Contact

The chief engineer of the Division of Water Resources for the Kansas State Board of Agriculture is responsible for the administration of laws related to water rights, water use, and water appropriations in Kansas.

David L. Pope, Chief Engineer, Division of Water Resources
Kansas Department of Agriculture
901 S. Kansas Avenue, 2nd Floor
Topeka, KS 66612
(913) 296-3717

How to Get a Water Right in Kansas

Persons wishing to use water for other than domestic use must file an application for a permit to appropriate with the chief engineer of the Division of Water Resources. (Unpermitted use is illegal, subject to civil and criminal penalties.) When a properly filled-out application is received in the Topeka, Kansas, headquarters, it is stamped with the date and time. That date and time become the priority date for that application should it ultimately be approved.

The two criteria the chief engineer must consider in evaluating applications are (1) whether the proposed use will impair an existing permit or water right and (2) whether the proposed use will adversely affect the public interest. One key factor in determining whether there will be an adverse affect on the public interest is whether a proposed use will meet safe yield. This standard refers to the long-term health of the system, basically looking to balance the amount of water being used under existing permits and water rights with the system's ability to restore its supply. If safe yield cannot be met, an application will be denied. Other factors come into play in evaluating applications, such as criteria for how closely together wells may be drilled.

Because most areas of the state are either near safe yield, fully appropriated, or overappropriated, the likelihood of obtaining approval of new applications is questionable.

Once an application is approved, six parameters are fixed: (1) priority date, (2) annual quantity, (3) maximum rate of diversion, (4) location of the point of diversion, (5) place of use, and (6) type of use. The first parameter cannot be changed. The second and third (quantity and rate) cannot be increased. The fourth, fifth, and sixth can only be changed by filing an application with the chief engineer and obtaining his approval. There are certain criteria for evaluating changed applications, such as the need to avoid impairment to existing permits and rights. Because many areas are no longer open to new permits, the division is receiving an increasing number of applications to change water rights to meet new needs. (For example, from irrigation to stock watering or from irrigation to municipal.)

Water rights are said to be perfected by the actual use of water as authorized by the permit. After the perfection time has expired, the diversion works are field-tested, and a certificate of appropriation is issued describing the extent to which the user perfected the right. The certificate is the final document in the process; it is of legal significance and should be filed with the local register of deeds. Permits and water rights may be transferred (bought, sold, leased, condemned), but any change in type of use, place of use, or point of diversion is subject to approval by the chief engineer.

Other Important Things to Know

A water right is a real property right that attaches to the land on which it is used. Therefore, the owner of the place of use owns the water right unless the right has been officially severed from the land by private written agreement or court order. The owner of the place of use, then, is responsible for maintaining the water right. For example, each water right owner must file a water use report with the division by March 1 of each year, documenting certain aspects of use during the previous year. Failure to file this report on time may subject the owner of the right to a $250 civil fine per water right.

Kansas water laws also provide for loss of a water right through nonuse. The law states that upon three successive years of nonuse, without due and sufficient cause for the nonuse, a water right is deemed abandoned. (In early 1996, the Kansas legislature was considering extending this period to five years.) The water right owner is entitled to an administrative hearing on the matter. The division has set forth regulations and policies defining what constitutes due and sufficient cause for nonuse.

Any person wishing to divert and transport water in a quantity of two thousand acre-feet or more over a distance of more than thirty-five miles from the point of diversion must make application to the chief engineer (as in all cases) and meet additional criteria set forth in the Kansas Water Transfer Act. The approval process involves an administrative hearing conducted by a hearing officer, followed by an opportunity to appeal to the three-member interagency water transfer panel, after which a party may appeal to district court. In evaluating applications for transfers, the hearing officer must consider a variety of factors, including:

• the present or reasonably foreseeable use

• the benefits to the state for either approving or not approving the transfer

• economic, environmental, public health, and welfare factors

• availability to the applicant of alternative sources of water

The applicant is also required to develop and implement an acceptable conservation plan.

Since water availability in Kansas is limited, the state emphasis has changed from one of water development to water conservation and management. Although management and regulatory decisions remain the exclusive authority of the chief engineer, local governmental units have formed to provide input and assistance. For example, five ground water management districts have formed in the south-central and western parts of the state. These districts develop management programs and recommend rules and regulations to the chief engineer to implement policies necessary to the conservation and management of ground water supplies. Mandatory metering, well-spacing restrictions, safe yield criteria, enforcement against water waste, and other programs have been used to protect ground water supplies.

The ground water management laws in Kansas also expand the chief engineer's authority to manage and regulate water use in areas of serious ground water decline. These areas are called Intensive Ground Water Use Control Areas. The chief engineer has designated several such areas, in which more restrictive measures now apply. Reductions in authorized quantity, multiyear allocation systems, mandatory metering, and conservation plans are examples of corrective control provisions that have been implemented in these areas.

Adjudication and Federal Reserved Water Rights in Kansas

Adjudication and federal reserved rights are aspects of western water law that have minimal application in Kansas. General adjudications are rare in light of Kansas's permit system. A small percentage of Kansas acreage is federal land, either federal military land or Indian reservation land. The governance over use of water on both types of federal land has not yet been an issue.

Protecting Kansas's Public Water Resources in the Twenty-first Century

Water Planning and Management.

The Kansas Water Office is responsible for water planning and coordinating for the state. The state water plan includes twelve river basins and sections on water management, conservation, quality, fish, wildlife, and recreation. The process for planning is continuous and updated annually. The state water plan must be approved by the Kansas Water Authority, which represents a broad spectrum of interests, before being submitted to the legislature and the governor. Policy recommendations found in the state water plan are presented to the chief engineer and legislature for approval. The legislature also determines funding for specific programs and projects.

Conservation and Prevention of Waste.

In 1992, the chief engineer instituted a new program called the Water Rights Conservation Program (WRCP). Under that program, the owner of a water right in good standing may enter into a contract with the division, in which the owner promises not to use any water under that right for a set number of years. In return, the division will consider enrollment as due and sufficient cause for nonuse, and the right will be protected from abandonment during the contract period. The purpose of the program is to encourage conservation of water.

The Water Appropriation Act prohibits waste of water and mandates that all use be reasonable and for the purpose authorized. In 1986, the legislature passed laws allowing the chief engineer to require water right holders and applicants to prepare and implement water conservation plans. The chief engineer may require conservation plans for all applications (for new permits or changes) filed after July 1, 1986.

Instream Flow.

Applications received after April 12, 1984, are considered to be junior in priority to any minimum desirable stream-flow requirements established by law for that source of supply. In the event that minimum desirable stream flow (MDS) seems seriously threatened, the Kansas Water Office has the responsibility of requesting the chief engineer to administer rights to protect the MDS.

Water Quality.

Although the chief engineer's duties do not include regulation of water quality, his decisions on water management include quality considerations. One of the two fundamental criteria for evaluating applications is that the proposed use not impair use under an existing right. The Water Appropriation Act lists certain factors as constituting impairment, including the unreasonable deterioration of the water quality at the user's point of diversion. In addition, the chief engineer has designated special water quality use control areas in which ground water is contaminated. New applications in that area are put on hold until the contamination cleanup project is completed. The reason for holding the new applications in those areas is that the pumping of a new well near the contaminated area can cause the contamination to spread.

Public Interest Criteria.

The Water Appropriation Act sets forth two fundamental criteria that all applications must meet in order to be approved. One criterion (described above) is that the proposed use must not impair a use under an existing water right. The second is that the proposed use will not prejudicially and unreasonably affect the public interest. The act sets forth certain factors for the chief engineer to consider in evaluating the impact on the public interest:

- established minimum desirable stream-flow requirements (levels set by law for particular streams and rivers)

- the area, safe yield, and recharge rate of the appropriate water supply

- the priority of existing claims of all persons to use the water of the appropriate water supply

- the amount of each claim to use water from the appropriate water supply

- all other matters pertaining to the issue of public interest

Recent regulations regarding the public interest require consideration of the quantity rate available and necessity to satisfy senior domestic rights from a stream, that senior water rights be protected from impairment by unreasonable concentrations of naturally occurring contaminants, and that a reasonable recharge of the alluvium (or other aquifer hydrologically connected to the stream) occur over the long term.

For More Information

Contact Division of Water Resources staff at the Topeka headquarters or one of the four field offices. The addresses are as follows:

Division of Water Resources
Kansas Department of Agriculture
901 S. Kansas Avenue, 2nd Floor
Topeka, KS 66612
(913) 296-3717

DWR Stafford Field Office
105 N. Main Street
Stafford, KS 67578
(316) 234-5311

DWR Garden City Field Office
214 Fulton Terrace
Garden City, KS 67846
(316) 276-2901

DWR Topeka Field Office
1643 SW 41st Street
Topeka, KS 66609-1250
(913) 267-6200

DWR Stockton Field Office
425 Main Street, Box 192
Stockton, KS 67669
(913) 425-6787

Coal Banks Landing, Upper Missouri, "Steamer Peninah." Summer 1880.
Haynes Foundation Collection, Montana Historical Society, Helena, Montana.

MONTANA

First Things First: What's the System?

Water allocation in Montana is based on the prior appropriation doctrine. Authority for water rights decisions is shared by the district court (including the water court) and the Water Rights Bureau of the Montana Department of Natural Resources and Conservation (DNRC).

Who to Contact

The Water Rights Bureau of the Montana Department of Natural Resources and Conservation is responsible for the administration, control, and regulation of water appropriated after June 30, 1973.

The Montana Water Court, a division of the district court, has exclusive jurisdiction for the general stream adjudication occurring on all pre–July 1, 1973, water rights. The water court focus is the examination and definition of all water rights developed before July 1, 1973.

All water rights forms required by the DNRC are available at each county clerk and recorder's office or at any of the eight regional offices of the Water Resources Division (listed at the end of this section). Additional publications are also available at little or no cost.

Montana Department of Natural Resources and Conservation
Water Rights Bureau
48 N. Last Chance Gulch
Helena, MT 59620
(406) 444-6610

How to Get a New Water Right in Montana

Generally, a new appropriation of water or the construction of a new diversion, withdrawal, impoundment, or distribution system requires that an application for a beneficial water use permit be filed with the nearest regional office of the DNRC. Permits are not required for ground water uses of less than thirty-five gallons per minute and ten acre-feet per year. After the well is completed, the user must obtain a Notice of Completion to acquire a water right for that ground water use.

Upon receipt of an application, the regional office reviews the application and sometimes makes a field investigation. Next, the department publishes notice in a newspaper and directly contacts other potentially affected water users. Time is then allowed for objections to be made. If objections cannot be resolved through informal discussions, a hearing examiner considers the evidence at an administrative hearing. A Proposed Order and Final Order are then issued.

Several criteria are considered in Montana when a new appropriation of water is sought:

• Is there unappropriated water in the source of supply at the proposed point of diversion at times, in the amount, and during the period of desired appropriation?

- Will the water rights of a prior appropriator be adversely affected?

- Are the proposed means of diversion, construction plans, and operation plans of the appropriation works adequate?

- Is the proposed use of water beneficial?

- Will the proposed use interfere unreasonably with other planned uses or developments for which a permit has been issued or for which water has been reserved?

- Does the applicant own the property or have the written consent of the owner of the property on which the water is to be put to beneficial use?

Other Important Things to Know

If a piece of land is sold or transferred from one landowner to another, any water rights attached to that land pass along to the new owner unless specifically stated otherwise. Although water rights can also be bought and sold separately from the land, the purpose of use, the point of diversion, place of use, or place of storage may not be changed without an authorization from the DNRC.

A water right under a permit can be abandoned if an appropriator stops using all or a portion of his/her water right with an intent to abandon it.

Adjudication and Federal Reserved Water Rights

A statewide general stream adjudication was initiated by the Montana legislature in 1979. Four water divisions were established, and the water court presides over each for the purpose of adjudicating all existing water rights. "Existing rights" are defined as rights to the use of water that would be protected under the law as it existed prior to July 1, 1973. This proceeding is intended to quantify all water rights based in state law and federal and tribal reserved water rights.

A Reserved Water Rights Compact Commission was established to negotiate compacts with federal agencies and Native American tribes in an effort to quantify reserved rights in Montana. Compacts will be incorporated into the statewide general stream adjudication process. Compacts have been successfully negotiated with the Ft. Peck and Northern Cheyenne Indian Reservations and the National Park Service. Examples include Glacier National Park, Yellowstone National Park, and the Little Bighorn Battlefield. If further compact negotiations are unsuccessful, federal and Indian reserved water rights will be determined in the state water court's adjudication process.

Over 201,000 claims were received by the water court by the April 30, 1982, deadline. These claims are being adjudicated gradually, basin by basin. Montana has eighty-five basins. The adjudication process involves several procedural steps, beginning with the filing of a claim with the DNRC and concluding with the issuance of a decree by the water court. The DNRC role in the process is to provide technical information and assistance to the water court.

The first issuance of a decree by the water court is termed either a Temporary Preliminary Decree or a Preliminary Decree. Temporary decrees are issued in basins containing federal reserved water rights where a compact has not been concluded. Such decrees contain all existing rights other than the reserved rights being negotiated. In these basins after a reserved water rights compact is negotiated, a Preliminary Decree will be issued as a second stage. It will include all rights in the Temporary Preliminary Decree along with all compacts concluded in the basins. A Preliminary Decree is issued at the outset during adjudication in basins without federal reserved rights.

The issuance of a Temporary Preliminary Decree or Preliminary Decree is followed by an objection period and a hearing if necessary. Once all objections have been resolved and decisions made, a Final Decree is entered. It may be appealed to the Montana Supreme Court. Upon resolution of appeals, a certificate of water right will be issued for every water right in the Final Decree.

At the time of this publication, forty-six basins in Montana have been decreed at the Temporary Preliminary Decree level. Approximately 117,000 claims remain to be decreed.

For information about issued decrees, objections, or hearings on pre–July 1, 1973, rights in the statewide adjudication, contact the Montana Water Court.

Montana Water Court
P.O. Box 879
Bozeman, MT 59771-0879
1-800-624-3270 (toll-free number within Montana only)
(406) 586-4364

Cutting ice from stream, Lewis & Clark County.

Protecting Montana's Public Water Resources in the Twenty-first Century

Water Planning and Management.

A State Water Plan is being prepared by the Department of Natural Resources and Conservation with extensive public involvement. It is required by state law to "set out a progressive program for the conservation, development, and utilization of the state's water resources" as well as to fulfill various other state water policy objectives.[23]

The State Water Plan provides a forum for all affected parties to collaboratively solve water management problems. It focuses on specific water management issues, whether of statewide or regional significance. Examples include instream flow protection, agricultural water use efficiency, and Milk River basin water shortages. The State Water Plan carries no authority to require compliance with its recommendations. Rather, through the creation and use of steering committees and advisory councils and the use of other techniques, it seeks to develop consensus solutions.

Although not the principal purpose, an important facet of the planning process is the role it plays in educating the public on water management issues and improving relationships among competing water interests. For more information on the Montana State Water Plan, contact the Water Management Bureau of the DNRC at (406) 444-6637.

Conservation and Prevention of Waste. Several methods are
used in Montana to encourage the conservation of water and prevent waste. One mechanism allows for basins in which water rights have been overappropriated to be "closed" to new appropriations. Basin closures may be accomplished administratively or legislatively.

To protect ground water from overdraft, "controlled ground water areas" may be designated by the Montana Board of Natural Resources upon receipt of a petition signed by at least twenty or one-fourth of the ground water users in a given area. A decision to make such designation is based on a number of criteria. Usually, facts and evidence are required to show that water withdrawals exceed aquifer recharge, significant conflict exists regarding

water rights and priorities in the area, ground water levels or pressures are declining excessively, or withdrawals threaten to cause degradation of water quality.

Instream Flow. Instream flows are
protected in Montana through several measures: a state water reservation process for future water uses, a pilot water-leasing program in selected basins, water conservation through a program encouraging the use of water measuring devices, and reservoir management. Further information on these topics may be obtained from the DNRC or the Montana Department of Fish, Wildlife and Parks.

Water Quality. The DNRC may
establish water quality standards for controlled ground water areas. Very large withdrawals of water are analyzed for their effects on water quality. Water use permits consider the water quality impacts of new appropriations on existing water rights.

Public Interest Criteria. The
export of Montana water to other states has been of historical concern to state residents. Water law now provides that water may be transported out of state if it is clearly determined that Montana will not be adversely affected.

DNRC WATER RESOURCES REGIONAL OFFICES

Billings Regional Office
1537 Avenue D, Suite 121
Billings, MT 59102
(406) 657-2105

Bozeman Regional Office
151 Evergreen, Suite C
Bozeman, MT 59715
(406) 586-3136

Glasgow Regional Office
630 Third Avenue South
P.O. Box 1269
Glasgow, MT 59230
(406) 228-2561

Havre Regional Office
1708 W. Second Street
P.O. Box 1828
Havre, MT 59501-1828
(406) 265-5516

Helena Regional Office
21 N. Last Chance Gulch
P.O. Box 201601
Helena, MT 59620-1601
(406) 444-0944

Kalispell Regional Office
3220 Highway 93 South
P.O. Box 860
Kalispell, MT 59903-0860
(406) 752-2288

Lewistown Regional Office
613 N.E. Main
P.O. Box 438
Lewistown, MT 59457-0438
(406) 538-7459

Missoula Regional Office
Holiday Village Plaza, Suite 105
P.O. Box 5004 (59806)
Missoula, MT 59801
(406) 721-4284

"James Gates House, 1888."
Solomon D. Butcher Collection, Nebraska State Historical Society.

NEBRASKA

First Things First: What's the System?

Historically, both riparian and prior appropriation systems have been used in Nebraska to allocate water rights. Today, riparian rights are infrequently relied upon. The riparian right in Nebraska allows some landowners whose property abuts a stream to use water from that source for beneficial purposes on, and only on, the adjacent land. The prior appropriation system began in 1895 and relies on a priority system dating to the earliest use of water. When shortages occur, water right holders with later priority dates must leave sufficient water in the source for those with earlier priority dates to use the full amount of water to which their right gives them title.

Who to Contact

The Nebraska Department of Water Resources is responsible for the issuance and administration of surface water rights and some ground water rights, including the required registration of all wells except those used solely for domestic purposes.

Bridgeport Office
729 Main Street
P.O. Box 787
Bridgeport, NE 69336-0787
(308) 262-0856

Cambridge Office
Luther Building, 401 Nasby
P.O. Box 426
Cambridge, NE 69022
(308) 697-3730

Crawford Field Office
P.O. Box 473
Crawford, NE 69339
(308) 665-1969

Lincoln Office
301 Centennial Mall South, 4th Floor
Lincoln, NE 68509-4676
(402) 471-2363

Norfolk Office
700 W. Benjamin, Country Club Plaza
P.O. Box 1451
Norfolk, NE 68702-1451
(402) 370-3377

North Platte Field Office
Craft State Office Building
200 S. Silber, Room 018
North Platte, NE 69101
(308) 535-8175

Ord Office
North Highway 11
P.O. Box 251
Ord, NE 68862
(308) 728-3325

How to Get a Water Right in Nebraska

To acquire a water right in Nebraska, one begins by filing an application (accompanied by a map) with the Department of Water Resources. If the application is eventually approved, the priority date is the date the application was submitted. Next, the department may publish a notice and determine if a hearing is needed. Before an application is approved, several criteria must be met:

• Is there unappropriated water, or is there sufficient water enough of the time?

• Is the application in the public interest?

• Would the application be detrimental to the public welfare?

• Would the application cause harm to any threatened or endangered species or its habitat?

• Will the water be put to beneficial use?

Assuming the above criteria are met, a water right may be approved.

Once a water right is obtained, it must be used at least once every three years. Failure to do so may be grounds for cancellation of the right. Water right holders are also expected to keep a record of their water use to ensure that they do not use more than their right specifies. The location of diversion shown on the water right is the only location from which water should be diverted. Finally, the water may only be used on the acreage specified by the water right.

Other Important Things to Know

Water users may make changes in their water rights if they win the approval of the Department of Water Resources. First, an application must be filed requesting the change. Such requests might involve relocating a point of diversion (pumping point) or transferring the water right to acreage not specified in the original water right. If the department determines that no harm will be done to others by the requested change, it will probably be approved.

Nebraska uses a constitutional preference system that operates secondarily to the "first in time, first in right" priority system. Domestic use is given preference over all other uses, and agriculture has preference over manufacturing and power uses. However, a junior preferred user does not have the right to water being used by a senior but subordinate user, unless that user is compensated for damages. To illustrate this principle, suppose that an agricultural water user with a 1960 priority date wants water from a hydroelectric power plant with a 1945 water right. The agricultural water user is out of luck unless willing to pay for power revenues lost through such a transfer.

The Ground Water Management and Protection Act gives authority to twenty-four natural resources districts to establish ground water control and management areas.[24] Well spacing, rotation of pumping, water allocation, and moratoriums on drilling are some of the management alternatives described in the act. Best management practices are also required to protect water quality.

Several control and management areas have been established in Nebraska to protect ground water resources by providing a means to regulate withdrawals and prevent the leaching of agricultural chemicals.

Adjudication and Federal Reserved Water Rights in Nebraska

One provision of Nebraska law is that the Department of Water Resources examine water appropriations to determine if water rights are being used and whether all diversions of water are legally valid. This process, which began in the late 1960s, is Nebraska's water adjudication procedure.

To accomplish adjudication, the state was divided into subbasins. Every water appropriation was investigated within approximately fifteen years, except those owned by irrigation districts and canal companies. In 1983, investigations of irrigation districts and canal companies were begun. This process continues to the present time.

The Nebraska adjudication process involves seven steps: (1) a records search, (2) investigation, (3) review of the investigation report, (4) public notice, (5) a hearing, (6) a decision, and (7) appeals and rehearing.

There are no federal or Indian reserved water rights in Nebraska.

Protecting Nebraska's Public Water Resources in the Twenty-first Century

Water Planning and Management. The Nebraska Natural Resources Commission is responsible for state water planning. In fulfilling its responsibilities, it collaborates with the twenty-four natural resources districts, which have taxing authority and manage soil and water resources at the local level.

Instream Flow. Instream flow rights may be obtained in a manner similar to other surface rights. They are given a priority date like all other rights and are regulated accordingly. Unlike other water rights in Nebraska, only a natural resource district or the Nebraska Game and Parks Commission may apply for instream flow rights. Only five instream rights have been granted as of the date of this publication.

Water Quality. The Nebraska
Department of Environmental Control
is responsible for the protection and
improvement of water quality. It administers point and nonpoint source pollution control programs for surface
water and ground water. Federal drinking water regulations are administered
by the Nebraska Department of Health,
which also conducts a Public Water
System program to provide safe water
through public systems. Individuals
with questions about safe drinking
water from private wells should contact the Department of Health.

Public Interest Criteria. Such
criteria are considered for certain
water rights.

For More Information

For further details regarding water
rights in Nebraska, contact Nebraska
Water Users, Inc., to obtain a copy of *A
Farmer's Guide to Water Rights.*

Nebraska Water Users, Inc.
2412 Highway 30 East, #3 Rovar Park
P.O. Box 820
Kearney, NE 68848-0820
(308) 234-9344
FAX (308) 237-2040

NEVADA

First Things First: What's the System?

The prior appropriation system is the basis of water appropriation in Nevada.

Who to Contact

The state engineer is responsible for appropriating, distributing, and managing water in Nevada. Those seeking to obtain a new water right or wanting to change an existing water right should contact:

Nevada State Engineer
Division of Water Resources
Capitol Complex
123 West Nye Lane, Room 246
Carson City, NV 89710
(702) 687-4380

The Nevada state engineer bears primary responsibility for administering and enforcing state water law and has broad discretionary power.

How to Get a New Water Right in Nevada

A new water right is created in Nevada by filing an application with the state engineer to appropriate water. A fee payment is required.

The procedure that follows the filing of an application to appropriate water includes four weeks of public notice in a newspaper near the point of diversion, a thirty-day protest period for those concerned about the new application, and a formal hearing to allow the applicant and opponent(s) to present their concerns.

The state engineer applies three basic criteria in assessing a new water right application:

- Is there unappropriated water in the proposed source?

- Will the proposed use impair existing rights?

- Does the proposed use threaten to prove detrimental to the public interest?

Nevada water laws do not define public interest in detail, and the state engineer can consider a variety of issues, depending on the application. If the state engineer approves an application, a permit is granted. Appeals to a district court are allowed for applications that are rejected. The permittee is given a specific time period to complete a proposed project and use the resource beneficially. Upon completion, the permittee must file proof of beneficial use with the state engineer. Proof must include the quantity of water developed, the extent of use, exact location of the diversion point, and other related information. A certificate of appropriation is issued upon satisfactory filing. Certificates of appropriation are said to have "certificated" or "perfected" status.

New ground water rights may be restricted in Nevada if they are determined to cause undue interference with preexisting wells. The state engineer has the authority to designate certain preferred uses when making ground water appropriations. Uses may include, but are not limited to, water for quasi-municipal, municipal, industrial, commercial, irrigation, mining, and stock watering purposes. Domestic use of ground water, which is defined as water for one house, is exempt from the provisions of the permitting process.

Other Important Things to Know

Water rights are real property in Nevada, so they may be transferred, bought, or sold. To change a water right, a process similar to seeking a new water right must be followed, beginning with an application.

Abandonment and forfeiture of water rights can occur in Nevada. Intent to stop using a water right is necessary for abandonment. Failure to use a water right for five consecutive years is grounds for forfeiture. Water lost through abandonment or forfeiture reverts to the public and becomes available for appropriation.

Adjudication and Federal Reserved Water Rights

An adjudication process in Nevada to determine the limit and extent of claims of vested water rights begins with field investigations and a hearing by the state engineer's office. Upon determination of the validity of the claims, an Order of Determination is submitted to the court. Further hearings and objections may be held by the judiciary. The court then issues a final decree, fully describing the limit and extent of all rights in that system.

"Wildhorse Dam, 1942."

The Northeastern Nevada Museum, Elko.

Protecting Nevada's Public Water Resources in the Twenty-first Century

Water Planning and Management.

The Division of Water Planning is responsible for investigating new sources of water, forecasting future supply and demand, formulating water policy, and providing information to political subdivisions and private businesses. New water projects may also obtain technical assistance from the division.

Conservation and Prevention of Waste.

Those who supply water for public consumption in Nevada are required by law to adopt water conservation plans. Each plan must include provision for public education, efficient water management to reduce leakage and mechanical problems, and a drought contingency plan to ensure a potable water supply. Analysis of the feasibility of charging variable rates to encourage conservation is also required. Another conservation measure includes standards for plumbing fixtures in new construction. Willful waste of water in Nevada is considered a misdemeanor.

Instream Flow.

No actual law protects instream flows in Nevada. However, wildlife are guaranteed access to springwater or seeping water. Wildlife watering has been acknowledged by judicial determination to be a beneficial use encompassed within recreational uses.

Water Quality.

The state engineer may consider water quality issues in making water appropriations.

NEW MEXICO

First Things First: What's the System?

Water rights in New Mexico are governed by the doctrine of prior appropriation. A state engineer, appointed by the governor and confirmed by the state senate, asserts broad authority for the supervision, measurement, appropriation, and distribution of the state's water.

Who to Contact

Applications for water permits may be filed with the state engineer's office in Santa Fe or in one of four district offices of the state engineer.

State Engineer Office
Water Rights Division
Bataan Memorial Building, Room 102
P.O. Box 25102
Santa Fe, NM 87504-5102
(505) 827-6120

How to Get a New Water Right in New Mexico

A permit is required to obtain a new surface water right in New Mexico. Permits are also required for ground water wells drilled in declared underground water basins. To protect prior appropriations, ensure the beneficial use of water, and maintain an orderly development of the state's water resources, the state engineer may establish declared underground water basins. As of June 30, 1993, thirty-two underground water basins were declared, encompassing 81 percent of the total land area of the state. Only well-drillers licensed by the state may drill, deepen, repair, or clean a water well within a declared underground water basin. No permit is required to drill wells outside declared basins. Changes in surface water or ground water use also require the filing of an application and approval by the state engineer.

Once an application for permit has been filed, notice is provided to the public, and protests to the granting of the application may be filed. A hearing before the state engineer or a designated hearing examiner is subsequently held to consider evidence and testimony on the disputed issues.

When considering an application for permit, the state engineer is required to consider:

• the existence of unappropriated water (if for a new appropriation)

• whether existing rights would be impaired

• whether the granting of the application would be contrary to the conservation of water within the state or detrimental to the public welfare of the state

The state engineer considers the evidence presented and issues findings and an order. These become final unless appealed to a district court within thirty days after receipt. The state engineer may approve the application in part or whole. A date is specified for completion of the proposed waterworks and beneficial use. Permits may also include conditions to prevent impairment of water rights.

Upon completion of the proposed water development as described on the permit, the appropriator files proof of completion of the works or well. The state engineer then issues a Certificate of Construction (for surface water) that attests to the location of the point(s) of diversion and the capacity of canals, ponds, or other works. After the water is fully used as described in the permit, the appropriator files proof of application of water to beneficial use and an inspection is made by the state engineer's staff. If all is in compliance with the permit, the state engineer issues a license to appropriate water.

Other Important Things to Know

If an appropriator in New Mexico fails to use water for four consecutive years, the state engineer may issue a notice and declaration of nonuse. If such water is not put back into beneficial use within one year after notice, that water reverts to the public. Forfeiture will not occur if circumstances are beyond the control of the appropriator.

New Mexico has an Interstate Stream Commission appointed by the governor. The state engineer is a member and its secretary as well as its executive officer. The commission is authorized to negotiate and administer interstate stream compacts to which New Mexico is a party. The commission may also investigate water supplies and take actions to develop, protect, and conserve the stream systems in the state.

Adjudication and Federal Reserved Water Rights

An adjudication of water rights in New Mexico involves the determination by the courts of all rights in a given stream system or declared basin. The state has adjudicated water rights since 1907 through a program of hydrographic surveys and adjudication lawsuits. Hydrographic surveys involve data collection to assist the court in the determination of the water rights to be awarded to each defendant (claimant). Individual claimants are given opportunity to present evidence of their water right claim to the court. Upon completion of the adjudication, the court issues a decree that defines the priority, amount, place, purpose, and periods of water use.

Protecting New Mexico's Public Water Resources in the Twenty-first Century

Water Planning and Management.
Municipalities, counties, state universities, and public utilities supplying water to municipalities and counties have statutory authority in New Mexico for a water use planning period of up to forty years from the date of application for a new appropriation or change in the exercise of an existing water right. During this time, they may acquire and hold unused water rights in amounts greater than current needs. In addition, regional water use plans have been funded and prepared.

Instream Flow.
New Mexico has no legislative or regulatory guidelines acknowledging instream flow as a beneficial use. However, the stream flow required at various points in the state is governed by interstate compacts, international treaties, federal court decrees, water rights conferred by the state under the doctrine of prior appropriation, and federal water development projects. In many situations, an incidental effect of these institutional constraints is an instream flow having important value in terms of recreation, fish and wildlife habitat, and aesthetics.

Public Interest Criteria.
Public welfare of the state and conservation of water within the state are criteria applied to water right permit applications and change applications in New Mexico. However, neither criterion is defined specifically in law or regulation.

NORTH DAKOTA

First Things First: What's the System?

North Dakota allocates water rights on the basis of the prior appropriation doctrine.

A water right permit is required for all water uses in North Dakota except for individual domestic or livestock purposes or for fish, wildlife, and other recreational uses, if those uses are for less than twelve and one-half acre-feet of water a year.

Who to Contact

The state engineer is the water rights administrator responsible for the appropriation, distribution, and management of water in North Dakota.

North Dakota State Water Commission
Office of the State Engineer
900 East Boulevard
Bismarck, ND 58505
(701) 224-2754

How to Get a New Water Right in North Dakota

To obtain a water right permit, an applicant must describe the proposed water development on an appropriate form and submit it with a fee payment to the state engineer. The application is reviewed for completeness and the applicant is then asked to notify (1) all landowners and all water permit holders within a radius of one mile from the proposed diversion point and (2) cities or public use water facilities within a specified area. Within sixty days, the applicant must verify that notice has been given by sending an affidavit of notice by certified mail. The date of receipt of the application becomes the priority date if the applicant complies within less than sixty days. Thereafter, the state engineer publishes notice in the area of the proposed appropriation once a week for two consecutive weeks. A hearing is then held by the state engineer to give all those with an interest in the application an opportunity to be heard.

The state engineer then evaluates the application in relation to the following criteria:

• The rights of a prior appropriator will not be unduly affected.

• The proposed means of diversion or construction are adequate.

- The proposed appropriation is in the public interest.

- The proposed use is beneficial.

In addition, the state engineer has authority to set conditions on permits to protect the rights of prior appropriators and the public interest. (See Public Interest Criteria in "Protecting North Dakota's Public Water Resources in the Twenty-first Century.")

An application that has been approved is referred to as a conditional water permit. Rejected applications may be appealed to the district court of the county in which the proposed point of diversion or storage is situated.

Once a permit has been issued, the appropriator is given a specific period of time (usually three years) to complete the project and put the water to beneficial use. On or before the spec-

Fargo, ND, 1897.
State Historical Society of North Dakota.

ified date, the state engineer inspects the works to verify that beneficial use has occurred and to determine the capacity, safety, and efficiency of the development. If all conditions are met and the works are satisfactory, a perfected water permit is issued. It describes the actual capacity of the works and specifies conditions.

Other Important Things to Know

For watercourses with insufficient supplies available to supply all competing permit applicants, the state engineer relies on the following order: (1) domestic use, (2) municipal use, (3) livestock use, (4) irrigation use, (5) industrial use, and (6) fish, wildlife, and other outdoor recreational uses. Competing applications are those received by the state engineer within ninety days of each other.

Conditional and perfected water rights may also be transferred to any parcel of land owned or leased by the permit holder. This requires the approval of the state engineer.

Changes in the point of diversion of water or purpose of water use can be made without affecting the priority date if approved by the state engineer. The approval is based on a determination that the proposed change will not adversely affect the rights of other appropriators. Changes in the purpose

of use are approved only for superior use, according to the following order of priorities: (1) domestic, (2) municipal, (3) livestock, (4) irrigation, (5) industrial, and (6) fish, wildlife, and other outdoor recreational uses.

Nonuse of a water right for three successive years can lead to loss of the right in North Dakota (i.e., forfeiture). A hearing is held to determine whether forfeiture has occurred, at which time the permit holder may appeal.

Several exceptions apply: unavailability of water, a justifiable inability to complete the waterworks, or evidence of other good and sufficient cause. As in other western states, water lost through forfeiture is subject to future appropriation.

Adjudication and Federal Reserved Water Rights

No general stream adjudication is occurring in North Dakota.

Issues involving federal reserved water rights have not yet been significant in North Dakota. However, two Indian reservations bordering state lakes may ultimately require determination of their federal reserved water rights. Furthermore, at least one of the tribes in North Dakota has proposed the adoption of a tribal water code. A first step to determining what water rights the tribe can administer will be the identification and quantification of those rights. When this occurs, the fundamental principles and attributes determined in federal case law will likely apply. (See "What Are Federal and Tribal Reserved Water Rights?" in Chapter Two for more detail.)

Protecting North Dakota's Public Water Resources in the Twenty-first Century

Water Planning and Management. The first statewide water plan, published in North Dakota in 1937, developed strategies to address specific water problems. The most recent State Water Plan, published in 1992, offers state and local decision-makers a thorough list of contemporary water management needs and public concerns; information on projects, programs, and water management issues; and short- and long-term schedules of recommended proposals designed to meet the state's future water needs. The product of extensive public involvement and technical review, the State Water Plan serves as an important tool for formulating state and local budgets and provides an educational resource and reference guide for water management. The plan is updated every five years or as directed by the State Water Commission or state engineer.

Conservation and Prevention of Waste. A water right can only be acquired for the amount of water put to beneficial use. Wasteful use is not beneficial.

Instream Flow. North Dakota law does not contemplate a water right for instream flows.

Water Quality. Water quality criteria with respect to usability are not considered in water appropriation procedures in North Dakota.

Public Interest Criteria. In determining whether or not a permit application is in the public interest, the state engineer considers the following: (1) the benefit to the applicant resulting from the proposed appropriation; (2) the effect of the economic activity resulting from the proposed appropriation; (3) the effect on fish and game resources and public recreational opportunities; (4) the effect of loss of alternate uses of water that might be made within a reasonable time, if not precluded or hindered by the proposed appropriation; (5) harm to other persons resulting from the proposed appropriation; and (6) the intent and ability of the applicant to complete the appropriation.

OKLAHOMA

First Things First: What's the System?

Surface water is considered public water in Oklahoma and is subject to the prior appropriation system, although this point is somewhat unsettled.[25] Ground water is considered private property that belongs to the owner of the surface land resource. It is subject to reasonable regulation by the state.

Who to Contact

A nine-member Oklahoma Water Resources Board appointed by the governor is responsible for the appropriation, distribution, and management of water in the state.

Oklahoma Water Resources Board
3800 N. Classen Blvd.
Oklahoma City, OK 73118
(405) 530-8800

How to Get a New Water Right in Oklahoma

The Stream Water Use Act requires that an application be filed before a water appropriator begins constructing a waterworks and before diverting or using water. Public notice is required once a week for two consecutive weeks

Panhandle—Extreme Western Oklahoma.

in a newspaper in the county where the diversion point is proposed and in the downstream county. An administrative hearing is also required. Any person or party whose interests are affected may appear at the hearing to protest the issuance of the permit.

Approval of the permit requires that the applicant establish the following:

• Unappropriated water is available in the amount requested.

• The applicant has a present or future need for the water, and the intended use is beneficial.

• The intended use will not interfere with domestic or existing appropriative uses.

• If the application is for the transportation of water for use outside the stream of origin, the proposed use must not interfere with existing or proposed beneficial uses within the stream system and the needs of water users there.

If the previous elements are met, the board approves the application and issues a permit to appropriate. Conditions may be imposed to protect prior water rights, flows, and other issues. The permit also includes conditions regarding the timely commencement and completion of the waterworks, actual diversion, and use

for the authorized purpose. Generally, the permittee is given seven years to perfect his/her appropriative water right. The vesting and perfection of the right occur at the time of, and to the extent of, the maximum amount of actual use by the seventh year. Continued use is required to retain the right once it has been perfected.

Ground water law in Oklahoma directs the board to conduct hydrologic surveys and investigations of each fresh ground water basin or subbasin to determine the maximum annual yield of water to be allocated to each acre of land overlying the basin or subbasin. With the exception of domestic uses, anyone seeking to use ground water must apply to the board before beginning to drill or before taking water. The procedure requires public notice once a week for two weeks in the appropriate county newspaper and actual notice by certified mail to all adjacent landowners.

Approval of a ground water permit application rests on satisfying the following criteria:

• The applicant owns or leases lands that overlie a fresh ground water basin or subbasin.

• The proposed use is beneficial.

• Waste by depletion or pollution will not occur.

Once these elements have been con-vincingly established, the board approves the application and issues a regular permit for the applicant's equal proportionate share of the maximum annual yield of the basin or subbasin.[26]

Other Important Things to Know

Stream and ground water permits may be transferred or assigned. However, if stream water has been authorized for irrigation uses, it remains attached to the irrigated land to which it is applied.

Adjudication and Federal Reserved Water Rights

Recently, Native Americans in Oklahoma have raised questions regarding the nature of their water rights. The Choctaw and Chickasaw Nations in southeast Oklahoma and the Osage in the northeast have challenged the right of the state to issue water rights.

The Choctaw and Chickasaw Nations have asserted that they own the water within their original tribal boundaries. The Osage Nation claims it owns all water and minerals in Osage County, and consequently the tribe claims all water bought and sold in the county should yield royalties to the tribe.[27] The Osages trace their claim to 1872, when they purchased the land and all mineral rights from the Cherokee Nation. Furthermore, the tribe seeks to have the county recognized as an Indian reservation, for they believe it will help people better understand their claims.

Because federal reserved water rights are distinctly different from state-based appropriative rights, resolution of these issues will take time.

Protecting Oklahoma's Public Water Resources in the Twenty-first Century

Water Planning and Management.
Presently, the Oklahoma Comprehensive Water Plan adopted in 1980 is being revised and updated.

Conservation and Prevention of Waste.
Waste of both stream water and ground water is prohibited by law.[28] Before permits can be issued, consideration of efficiency of use occurs on a case-by-case basis.

Instream Flow.
In order to issue a permit to appropriate stream water, the board must determine whether water is available. An amount necessary to protect existing appropriative uses and domestic use (ten acre-feet/household/year) is subtracted from the amount available.

Also, in determining the amount of water available for appropriation, the rules of the board set out a presumption that unappropriated flow quantities that are available less than 35 percent of the time on an average annual basis will not be considered to be water available for appropriation.

The rules of the board provide additional factors to be considered when an applicant seeks to appropriate stream water from "scenic river areas"[29] or streams designated as "outstanding resource waters,"[30] in order to ensure that appropriate instream flows are protected.[31]

Water Quality.
Water quality in Oklahoma is protected by state law and board rules submitted to the Environmental Protection Agency under Section 301 of the Clean Water Act.

Public Interest Criteria.
State law does not directly address public interest. However, considerations regarding waste and possible riparian claims for instream flows may lead to the same result.

OREGON

First Things First: What's the System?

Oregon's water rights system is based upon the doctrine of prior appropriation. However, until enactment of Oregon's water code in 1909, the state recognized riparian water rights under certain circumstances. Remnants of riparian water rights exist only in unadjudicated basins.

Water use in Oregon is administered by a statewide watermaster corps that distributes all surface water and ground water according to "water rights of record," which may include completed water use permits, certificates of water right, and court decrees. Also, water rights of record include certain **de minimis** exempt uses.

Who to Contact

The Oregon Water Resources Department and Water Resources Commission are the key water allocation entities in the state. The commission is a citizen body responsible for determining state water policy. It also acts as a board of directors for the department. The department serves as the commission's staff and is responsible for implementing water policy.

Oregon Water Resources Department
3850 Portland Road N.E.
Salem, OR 97310
(505) 378-8455

How to Get a New Water Right in Oregon

In order to develop a new use of ground water or surface water in Oregon, a permit application and fee payment must be submitted to the Water Resources Department. Before a water right certificate is issued, the applicant must provide a map prepared by a certified water right examiner (CWRE). Any professional engineer or land surveyor in Oregon may be certified after passing an examination.

Oregon's water rights application process was substantially revised in 1995. Upon receipt of an application, the Water Resources Department reviews it for completeness and, if necessary, returns it to the applicant for completion or issues a refund. Upon completion, the application is given a tentative priority date and then reviewed according to several statutory criteria. Public notice of the application is made to allow for comments. A Proposed Final Order is prepared and distributed to the applicant and other interested parties. Public notice of the Proposed Final Order is also given.

Forty-five days are allowed for protests to be made. If no protests are made, a Final Order is prepared within sixty days of the protest deadline.

Protests require a $200 fee payment. If protests are filed, the director of the Water Resources Department may or may not hold a contested case hearing, prior to making a final determination regarding the application. The applicant may also protest the Proposed Final Order and request a contested case hearing, in which case the director is required to hold it. Contested case hearings are generally held under the following circumstances: at the request of the applicant; when the facts associated with an application are in dispute; if the application raises public interest questions, big policy issues, or high public concern. Following a contested case hearing, a Proposed Order is issued by the hearings officer.

Final Orders are issued by the director. If exceptions to a Final Order are filed, they are referred to the Water Resources Commission to determine their validity. Upon issuance of the Final Order with permit, development of the water must be initiated within one year. In addition, deadlines for completion of water development are specified on the permit. Development must generally be completed within five years. At completion, a final proof survey is made and submitted to the Water Resources Department. If the director is satisfied that all conditions of the permit have been met, a certificate of water right is granted.

Other Important Things to Know

All water use in Oregon is attached to the land where it is used. Changes in the point of water diversion, place of use, and nature of use must have prior approval. Those seeking transfers of their water rights must apply to the Water Resources Department. If such a transfer will not injure an existing water right, it will probably be approved.

Water rights in Oregon may be voluntarily abandoned by the owner or forfeited by five consecutive years of nonuse.

Applications to use ground water in Oregon are examined for their potential to interfere with existing wells, surface water claims, or existing rights to water for its thermal characteristics. To prevent excessive declines in ground water levels, to avoid interference between surface water and ground water users, and to stop water quality degradation, the Water Resources Commission may declare certain areas "critical ground water areas." In these areas, water use restrictions and preferences may apply.

If an individual seeks to use water outside the **basin of origin**, a comprehensive evaluation of the potential effects of such use on the basin of origin is required at the applicant's expense.

The Oregon Departments of Environmental Quality, Fish and Wildlife, and Parks and Recreation may also file applications for instream flow rights to protect stream flows for public uses.

Adjudication and Federal Reserved Water Rights

Water uses that began in Oregon before February 24, 1909, are verified, quantified, and documented by an adjudication process in the circuit court of the county where the water is used. Water uses that began before this time are said to be vested unless such rights have since been forfeited through nonuse. Pre-1909 water rights have been adjudicated in about two-thirds of Oregon.

The local circuit courts or director of the Water Resources Department may initiate river basin adjudications. A "proof of claim" is filed with the department. Claims are reviewed, each development is examined, hearings are held, and a finding of fact and order of determination are then filed with the county circuit court where the water use occurs.

Claims may be contested by those whose interests would be affected. Any person who claims an interest in the same water source is made a party to the claim and is bound by the adjudication.

The circuit court reviews the order of determination, affirms or modifies it, and enters a final judgment called a decree. The decree serves as final determination of all pre-1909 and federal reserved water rights in that river or stream basin. Individual certificates are then issued to water claimants by the department, according to terms described in the decree.

Protecting Oregon's Public Water Resources in the Twenty-first Century

Water Planning and Management. The Oregon state legislature determines most water use policy. The legislature has delegated the administration of Oregon's water law to a seven-member Water Resources Commission, appointed by the governor. The director of the Water Resources Department is responsible

for administering and implementing the various water policies developed by these two bodies.

The Water Resources Commission has developed programs for the coordination of water development and use, protection of minimum stream flows, stream basin planning, drought management, and enforcement of water rights. Because of its stream basin planning authority, the Water Resources Commission may restrict water uses within a basin or withdraw a source from further appropriation.

Conservation and Prevention of Waste.
Conservation and waste prevention are important aspects of Oregon water law. All water users are required to eliminate waste, and certain larger water users must prepare conservation plans. Any water right holder may submit a conservation plan to the Water Resources Commission; if the plan is approved, a percentage of the conserved water will be retained by the user. Water rights exchanges may be permitted if they foster conservation.

Instream Flow.
Instream flows are protected in Oregon in several ways. Private persons having water rights may convert their rights to instream flow. However, new applications for establishing instream flow rights may only be acquired by the Departments of Environmental Quality, Fish and Wildlife, and Parks and Recreation.

Instream flow rights are considered water held in trust by the department for public uses. Public uses include recreation, conservation, fish and wildlife maintenance and habitat, other ecological values, pollution abatement, and navigation. Instream flow rights may not impair existing permitted or vested rights. These instream water rights may be subordinated to certain other uses, such as needs for multipurpose storage or municipal or hydroelectric uses. Applications for instream flow rights involve a public interest review.

Public Interest Criteria.
Review of applications to appropriate water includes consideration of whether a proposed use would be detrimental to or impair the public interest. In making such determinations, the Water Resources director examines the "highest use" of the water: the maximum economic development of the water; how the water may be controlled for such purposes as drainage, sanitation, or flood control; the amount of water available; the prevention of wasteful, uneconomic, impractical, or unreasonable uses; and the protection of existing rights.

SOUTH DAKOTA

First Things First: What's the System?

Prior appropriation became the basis for allocating surface water in South Dakota before it became a state, and ground water followed in 1955. Prior appropriation remains the foundation of water rights today with the exception of some domestic uses.[32]

Who to Contact

Authority to issue water permits of all types in South Dakota rests with a seven-member Water Management Board, appointed by the governor. A chief engineer and the Water Rights Program complete review and technical assessment of applications as described below.

Department of Environment and Natural Resources
Water Rights Program
523 East Capitol
Pierre, SD 57501-3181
(605) 773-3352

How to Get a New Water Right in South Dakota

Water permits and water rights are acquired through an application procedure that begins with the filing of the proper forms obtained from the chief engineer. The form requires informa-tion about the water source, the amount of water to be claimed, location of diversion points, the type of use, and the annual time period of use. A map of the project, fee payment, and relevant supplemental information (e.g., the storage capacity of a proposed pond or reservoir or a well driller's test hole log) may be required.

The permit application is reviewed by the staff of the Water Rights Program and a report is prepared. The chief engineer reviews the report and prepares a recommendation to approve, deny, or defer the application based on the following criteria:

- Reasonable probability exists that unappropriated water is available.

- The proposed diversion can be developed without unlawful impairment of existing rights.

- The proposed use is a beneficial use.

- The proposed use is in the public interest.

A notice of hearing, describing the application and the chief engineer's recommendation, is then published in each county where the water is to be diverted or used. If no petition opposing the application is filed and the recommendation is to approve the application, the chief engineer may issue a water permit on behalf of the

Water Management Board. If petitions opposing the application are filed, the application is considered during a contested case hearing before the Water Management Board.

The board may accept, reject, or modify the chief engineer's recommendation and issue the permit subject to terms, conditions, restrictions, and other limitations to protect the public interest. Findings of fact, conclusions of law, and a final decision are then prepared by the board's attorney. After a comment period, the board considers adopting the findings, conclusions, and final decision. A water permit is issued if the board's decision is not appealed.

The water permit includes information from the application, qualifications attached by the engineer or board, and specified time periods for construction and beneficial use of the water. Five years from the date of approval are normally granted for construction of waterworks, and four additional years are given to put the water to beneficial use.

Upon completion of the project and beneficial use, an on-site inspection is conducted to determine that all is in compliance with the permit requirements. A water license is then issued for the project, and the permit becomes a water right.

Other Important Things to Know

The Water Rights Program also requires permit applications for individuals or other entities seeking to (1) amend existing water use permits or rights, (2) reserve water for future use, (3) control flooding or modify a watercourse, and (4) claim vested water rights. The same procedure required for new water use permits is followed for processing these types of applications.

Applications may also be filed to amend water permits or water rights to alter the types of water use or change the location of use. A diversion point may be relocated from the permitted diversion point without publishing notice if the change doesn't interfere with existing diversions. An irrigation water permit or right may only be transferred from irrigation use to domestic use or to use within a water distribution system. No change may increase the rate of water diversion or volume of water appropriated under the original permit or right, and changes may not impair existing rights. Water permits may be canceled for failure to construct the systems within the time period specified on the permit. Failure to use water beneficially may result in cancellation of the permit or forfeiture of a water right. Three years of nonuse of all or any part of the water subjects the permittee or water right holder to possible forfeiture of the right. Certain legal excuses for nonuse of water are accepted: unavailability of water to satisfy a permit or right, legal proceedings that prevent the use of water, waste resulting from use of the water under existing climatic conditions, and participation in an acreage reserve or other federal production quota program.

Adjudication and Federal Reserved Water Rights

No general stream adjudication is occurring in South Dakota. No federal reserved water right claims have been asserted, and no policy has been formulated.

Protecting South Dakota's Public Water Resources in the Twenty-first Century

Water Planning and Management. There is a water planning process in South Dakota. The state water plan is divided into two areas—the state water facilities plan and the state water resources management system. The facilities plan addresses smaller projects such as municipal or rural water supplies, wastewater facilities, ground water contamination, and other types of pollution prevention. Growing emphasis is being placed on watershed management to address nonpoint source pollution.

The water resources management system typically includes large, costly water projects that require federal as well as state funding. These projects include rural water systems, flood control, hydrology studies, and irrigation projects. Development of large rural water systems supplied from the Missouri River continues to be an area of emphasis.

Conservation and Prevention of Waste. The state water plan includes projects to conserve water resources. As an example, the Belle Fourche Irrigation Project is a large Bureau of Reclamation project that is being rehabilitated to allow more efficient use of water. State statute prohibits the waste or unreasonable use of water. In accordance with statute, permits to appropriate water are often issued with qualifications concerning conservation and prevention of waste of water. State statute also requires that owners of flowing wells control the wells to prevent waste of water.

Instream Flow. State law allows anyone to file an application to appropriate water for instream flows. To date, only two permits have been issued for instream flows to support fisheries and recreation. The first permit was approved in 1941. Appropriative water uses are also subject to bypassing stream flows to accommodate downstream domestic uses such as livestock water. Domestic

use of water in South Dakota takes precedence over appropriative uses.

Instream flow concerns may also be addressed as a public interest issue during a hearing on an application to appropriate water for a consumptive use. In two instances, permits to appropriate water were denied primarily to maintain adequate flows to protect a trout fishery.

Water Quality.

Water quality criteria are considered from the standpoint of what happens to any wastewater generated by a beneficial use of water. Permits to appropriate water are often qualified to address the disposal or storage of wastewater to ensure compliance with applicable federal and state laws.

Typically, the impact to the water quality of a water source by removing water from the source is not considered. This issue has been raised and addressed on occasion through the public interest avenue.

Public Interest Criteria.

Public interest is one of four criteria that must be considered and satisfied prior to issuance of a permit to appropriate water. However, public interest is not defined by statute or rule.

During a contested case hearing, the Water Management Board typically gives interested parties wide latitude in presenting issues of public interest. Examples of public interest concerns include odors, property values, water quality issues, aesthetics, and fisheries.

Typically, consideration of the public interest by the Water Rights Program during review of a permit application involves determining whether the other three criteria are met in order for a permit to be issued. The other three criteria are (1) availability of unappropriated water, (2) unlawful impairment to existing rights, and (3) beneficial use. Typically, if these criteria are met, the chief engineer makes the determination that the application is in the public interest and recommends approval of the application. The public then has the opportunity to intervene and raise other public interest issues for the board's consideration.

TEXAS

First Things First: What's the System?

The prior appropriation doctrine applies only to surface water in Texas. The **right to capture** principle is the basic legal principle applied to ground water appropriation.

Who to Contact

The Texas Natural Resource Conservation Commission (TNRCC) is responsible for managing surface water appropriation in Texas. The commission is a three-person body appointed by the governor and approved by the state senate. Each member serves a six-year term, and new appointments are made at two-year intervals.

Texas Natural Resource Conservation Commission
Agriculture and Watershed Management Division
Surface Water Uses Section
P.O. Box 13087, Mail Code 160
Austin, TX 78711
(512) 239-4609

The state of Texas has no comprehensive authority over ground water appropriation. Instead, underground water conservation districts, subsidence districts, and some critical area designations have been created that have the power to limit appropriation of ground water within their boundaries.

How to Get a New Water Right in Texas

A water right is required for any diversion, impoundment, or use of surface water from any stream or watercourse in Texas.[33]

A landowner or business seeking to obtain a new water right must first complete the proper application form provided by the TNRCC. Another format may also be used as long as the required information is present. Upon receipt of the application and a fee payment, commission staff review the application (within ten days) to see that it is administratively complete. If so, it is declared and processed. If not, the applicant is notified and given thirty days to provide additional information.

The next stage involves technical and environmental review by commission staff. The following criteria guide the staff's assessment and final recommendation to the commission:

• Is there sufficient unappropriated water at the proposed point of diversion to satisfy the applicant's demand?

• Has the applicant demonstrated a need or beneficial use for the amount of water requested?

• Will this request have any impact on existing water rights?

• Will the proposed project have any environmental impacts?[34]

Texas law also requires that the Texas Parks and Wildlife Department be given a copy of the new application for review and comment.

The applicant bears responsibility for supporting his/her application with appropriate data, studies, or information. Commission staff may require additional information to make their final determination. If impacts are determined to exist, staff may propose mitigation plans, special conditions, or term limitations to offset or alleviate such possible conditions. All applicants for a new water right are required to submit conservation plans with their applications to ensure that the water they request will be used beneficially.

Upon completion of staff review, the application is placed upon the commission's agenda, and all water right holders in the affected basin are notified of the application. The applicant must also publish notice in a newspaper in the area of the proposed water use.

An opportunity is given for affected parties to protest the application and request a hearing. If such protest occurs, the commission refers the case to an administrative judge as a contested case. Evidence is given, testimony is taken, and all parties may participate. At the conclusion of the hearing, the examiner issues a recommendation (findings of fact and conclusions of law). These are given to the commission for consideration at the first available time. The commission then considers the application and recommendation in a public hearing. All parties are given notice and opportunity to speak. A final decision is then made by the commission, and approved applications are given a permit.

The water right becomes vested in Texas "to the maximum extent the permittee has used the right in any one year."

Other Important Things to Know

Water rights are real property in Texas. As such, they can be bought, sold, or conveyed by deed. When such transactions are made, the TNRCC must be notified through the filing of an appropriate form describing the change in ownership.

Water right holders may also file applications to change the place of use, purpose of use, diversion point, or diversion rate. This requires application for amendment to an existing permit. Staff evaluation applies many of the same criteria used for approving a new water use permit.

Water rights can be canceled or abandoned in Texas. Cancellation is based on the maximum beneficial use in the last ten years. It may involve cancellation of a portion of a water right or an entire water right. Abandonment is difficult to prove and usually occurs voluntarily. Following abandonment or cancellation of a water right, that water reverts to the public.

Adjudication and Federal Reserved Water Rights

A statewide adjudication of all surface water rights in Texas was established in 1967. All areas of the state have been adjudicated, except for a small portion of the Rio Grande River near El Paso. The adjudication process involves an administrative proceeding undertaken by the TNRCC, with review by the Texas judiciary.

Protecting Texas's Public Water Resources in the Twenty-first Century

Water Planning and Management. The Texas Water Development Board (TWDB) has an ongoing long-range water planning process. Every two years, a review is required to determine if there have been "significantly changed conditions" that might necessitate attention or revision of the plan. At a minimum, every two years conditions are examined, and the board is advised about the condition of water resources at that time. At this writing, a consensus-based approach is being used to coordinate planning among the three key state agencies sharing water management responsibility in Texas: the TNRCC, the TWDB, and the Texas Parks and Wildlife Department. Public representation involving all user and affected groups is also part of the planning process through technical advisory committees targeting (1) water demands, supplies, and drought management; (2) water quality; and (3) ecological water needs.

Conservation and Prevention of Waste. The TNRCC and TWDB have jointly developed water conservation rules. Together, the agencies offer a wide array of technical assistance for improving municipal, industrial, and agricultural conservation.

Because of water scarcity, numerous projects, such as Trans-Texas, promote reuse by municipalities where possible. The Trans-Texas Water Program is organized into three study areas that include the major water demand centers of Houston, Austin, Corpus Christi, and San Antonio. Water availability, which varies considerably across the region, is the major focus of this planning effort. It has been forecast that by the year 2040, water shortages will exist in five of the eight river basins included in the overall study area. Three basins, however, are predicted to have surpluses.

The overall goal of the program is to identify the most cost-effective and environmentally sensitive strategies for meeting the current and future water needs of the study area. Once determined, alternatives will be assessed in terms of technical feasibility, cost, and environmental acceptability. This program also promotes transference of water into water-poor areas.

The Texas Water Bank was created by the 73rd Texas legislature to allow for and assist in voluntary transfer of water rights between willing buyers and sellers. The transfer may be either temporary or permanent and in most instances will require a permit modification from the TNRCC. The bank is a program of the TWDB, which facilitates the marketing and transfer of water and water rights through provision of information describing both availability and needs for water in the state.

Instream Flow. Instream flow protection is evaluated as a part of an environmental assessment on an application for a water right. This is in conjunction with the Texas Parks and Wildlife Department to ensure that aquatic habitat and instream needs are protected. This is usually in the form of restrictions on a water right. (For example, no diversion may occur unless stream flow is above the annual median flow.) Instream flow and other environmental criteria are being further refined in the three-agency consensus water planning process.

Water Quality. Permitting for discharges of wastewater in Texas is a separate process; however, there is interaction among various groups to allow for beneficial uses or reuse of available water (discharges). Some permits for use are based wholly upon presence of effluent in the stream. Dilution and wasteload factors are considered in water quality permitting.

Public Interest Criteria. The TNRCC may consider public interest criteria when reviewing new water use applications. However, Texas water law does not specifically define what public interest criteria may be applied.

UTAH

First Things First: What's the System?

The prior appropriation doctrine is the basis of water appropriation in Utah.

Who to Contact

The state engineer is responsible for administration of water rights in Utah, including the appropriation, distribution, and management of state water.

Utah Division of Water Rights
1636 W. North Temple Street
Salt Lake City, UT 84116-3156
(801) 538-7240

How to Get a New Water Right in Utah

A new water right is obtained by filing the proper application form and paying a fee to the state engineer. The application requires a description of the proposed water development.

The application is reviewed for completeness and adherence to required policies. A legal notice is prepared and published for two weeks in a newspaper near the proposed water source. A twenty-day protest period follows the advertisement, allowing time for anyone who has an interest in the application to protest. If protests are filed, a hearing is generally conducted. This allows the applicants and objectors opportunity to present their data and information to the state engineer in support of their positions. Applications not acted upon are referred to as "unapproved."

The state engineer applies the following criteria in assessing new applications:

• Is there unappropriated water in the proposed source?

• Will the proposed use impair existing rights or interfere with more beneficial uses of the water?

• Is the proposed plan physically and economically feasible?

• Does the applicant have the financial ability to complete the proposed works?

• Was the application filed in good faith and not for purposes of speculation or monopoly?

• Will it unreasonably affect public recreation or the natural stream environment?

• Will it be detrimental to the public welfare? Public welfare is not defined specifically by state law.

The state engineer can consider different issues, depending on the application. Water quality issues, in recent times, have begun to be considered.

Approved applications may have conditions imposed upon them by the state engineer to protect prior water rights, to better define the extent of the right, or to address other issues. For example, an application might be approved pending acquisition of required permits from other regulatory agencies or requiring minimum stream-flow bypasses. When an application is approved it is referred to as an approved application.

Approved applications are given for a specific period of time (usually three years) to develop the water use. Upon completion of the project and beneficial use, the applicant must file proof of appropriation with the state engineer.[35] If the proof of appropriation is accepted by the state engineer, a certificate of appropriation is issued to finalize the application process. The water right is then said to be certificated or perfected.

Other Important Things to Know

Applications for a new water right are considered personal property; thus they may be bought and sold using a conveyance or assignment. When water rights are perfected, they are considered real property and must be conveyed by deed to the new owner.

Landowners may also change the purpose of use of a water right, the point of diversion, and place of use. To do so requires filing a changed application describing the planned modifications with the state engineer. The same criteria used to assess a new water right application are applied, along with two additional considerations:

• Does the proposed water use, both the quantity diverted and consumed, exceed historical levels?

• Are intervening rights impaired as a result of the change?

In many areas of Utah, water is fully appropriated, so future uses of water require that existing water rights be transferred.

Abandonment and forfeiture of water rights can occur in Utah. Intent is the criterion used to determine that abandonment has occurred, and no time period is required by law. Forfeiture may be said to occur if a water right is not used for five years. Water lost through abandonment or forfeiture returns to the public for future water appropriations.

Adjudication and Federal Reserved Water Rights

About two-thirds of Utah has been or is currently being adjudicated. The general adjudication of water rights in the state is handled through the state district court. The process requires that the state engineer investigate and survey water uses within a given basin and accept all water users' claims to a water right. The claims are evaluated and the state engineer issues a recommendation to the state court. The adjudication procedure has been used to resolve water rights conflicts and to update water rights records.

Protecting Utah's Public Water Resources in the Twenty-first Century

Water Planning and Management.
State water planning began in Utah in 1963 at the direction of the state legislature. Today, the State Water Plan is an ongoing process to establish and implement the state's policy on water management. The plan blends the input of state and federal agencies and private contributors into a framework for the future. The goal of the state water planning process is to provide water to meet the changing needs of present and future generations.

Agriculture, municipal and industrial water pollution control, recreation, wildlife, flood control, and drought response are all recognized as important components of the State Water Plan. As of 1990, the plan consisted of twenty sections that address such topics as demographics and economic future, water supply and use, state and federal water resources funding programs, agricultural water conservation and development, development and management of drinking water supplies, water pollution control, disaster and emergency response, fisheries and water-related wildlife, recreational aspects of water development, industrial water use, and ground water.

Public Interest Criteria. The

right to appropriate surplus and unappropriated water in Utah may be suspended by the governor upon the recommendation of the state engineer if the welfare of the state (or the needs of agriculture) demands that such action be taken. Furthermore, the state engineer may not approve new water use applications if they are deemed to be detrimental to the public welfare.

Conservation and Prevention of Waste. The state engineer may

require that water delivery systems be repaired or constructed so as to prevent waste or loss of water.

Section 10 of the Utah State Water Plan covers four agricultural water conservation issues, including irrigation water development, management competition for agricultural land and water, agricultural-induced nonpoint pollution, and use of saved water. Nine additional conservation issues are addressed in Section 17, including water supply efficiency, dual water systems, irrigation water development and management, home and municipal water savings and pricing, water reuse, timing of water supply for landscaping, and water education.

Water Quality. Repair or construc-

tion of water delivery systems to prevent water contamination or pollution may be required by the state engineer. Furthermore, ground water permits may not be approved if they are determined to adversely affect the water quality of an aquifer.

The Utah Water Pollution Control Act regulates the discharge of pollutants into Utah waters. The Utah Water Quality Board implements the rules, regulations, policies, and ongoing planning processes necessary to prevent, control, and abate new or existing water pollution. This is carried out through the Division of Water Quality.

Instream Flow. The Utah Divisions

of Wildlife Resources and Parks and Recreation may acquire existing water rights and file (change) applications for instream flow rights. Such applications must include information demonstrating the necessity for instream flows and the benefits to be derived for fisheries and recreation. Purchase, lease, agreement, gift, exchange, and contributions may also be means whereby these state agencies acquire water for instream flow protection. Such rights may only be acquired for the preservation or propagation of fish, public recreation, or the reasonable preservation or enhancement of the natural stream environment.

WASHINGTON

First Things First: What's the System?

The prior appropriation doctrine is the basis of water appropriation in the state of Washington. All unappropriated water belongs to the state.

Who to Contact

The Washington Department of Ecology is responsible for the appropriation, distribution, and management of the state's surface water and ground water resources. Four regional offices exist to provide water users access to the department's services.

Department of Ecology
Northwest Regional Office
3190 160th Avenue SE
Bellevue, WA 98006-5452
(206) 649-7000

Department of Ecology
Central Regional Office
106 S. Sixth
Yakima, WA 98902-3387
(509) 575-2597

Department of Ecology
Southwest Regional Office
5751 Sixth Ave.
Lacey, WA 98503
Mail: P.O. Box 47775
Olympia, WA 98504-7775
(206) 407-6300

Department of Ecology
Eastern Regional Office
4601 N. Monroe, Suite 202
Spokane, WA 99205-1295
(509) 456-2734

How to Get a New Water Right in Washington

Landowners or others seeking to divert water from surface water or ground water sources in Washington must file an application and pay a fee at the appropriate regional office of the Department of Ecology.

The Department of Ecology reviews new applications for completeness, then sends the applicant a legal notice to be published twice in a newspaper of central circulation in the county where the water is to be diverted and used. The public notice advertises the new application and provides thirty days for protests to be filed. After final publication, the applicant must return the original Affidavit of Publication to the department.

At the conclusion of the thirty-day protest period, the department conducts an investigation of the application. This usually includes a field investigation to verify the information on the application, take any needed measurements, ensure that the project is reasonable, and investigate any protests.

The Department of Ecology may not approve an application unless the following findings are made:

• The water is available.

• The intended use is beneficial.

• Issuance of a water right will not impair existing water rights.

• The public interest will not be detrimentally affected.

A Report of Examination is issued by the department describing the recommendation for approval or denial of the application. Approved water rights may have special provisions or conditions, such as meeting minimum instream flow requirements for fish, wildlife, and aesthetics before water is withdrawn. If an application is denied or a condition is disputed, the decision may be appealed to Washington's Environmental Hearing Office, Pollution Control Hearings Board. Third parties may also appeal. If all conditions have been satisfied and no appeal has been filed, a Permit to Appropriate Public Waters is issued. Although this is not an actual water right, it allows a reasonable time frame for the construction of necessary waterworks and specifies a final date by which the water must be put to beneficial use.

Upon completion of necessary construction and beneficial use of the water, the permittee must file a Proof of Appropriation with the department and pay a certificate fee.[36] A site investigation may be conducted to verify that all conditions have been satisfied as claimed.

A Certificate of Water Right is then issued if all conditions have been met. This certificate is recorded with the auditor's office of the county in which the water right is located and at the Department of Ecology. Thereupon, it becomes the legal record of the water right and is forwarded to the applicant.

Ground water permits are not required for stock watering, irrigation of up to half an acre of lawn or noncommercial garden, single or grouped domestic uses totaling less than five thousand gallons per day, or industrial uses of up to five thousand gallons per day. Rights to these uses are established even though no certificate or permit is issued. However, the Department of Ecology may require such unpermitted water users to provide information on the means and quantity of their withdrawal.

Other Important Things to Know

Certain conditions must be met before a water right holder is entitled to change the purpose of use, place of use, or point of diversion. First, an application must be filed with the Department of Ecology. Public notice must be given. The proposed change must be determined not to adversely affect existing water rights. If these conditions are satisfied, the department authorizes the change with a specific construction schedule and then issues a certificate that serves as a record of the change.

Recent legislation in Washington allows for water rights to be transferred to the state through purchase or donation while maintaining the original priority date. Water rights can also be acquired in Washington through purchase or, rarely, condemnation. Condemnation proceedings are initiated in a superior court to condemn an "inferior use of water for a superior use." Water rights are attached to the land but may be separated and attached to other land through a change of place of use.

Water rights may also be abandoned or relinquished (forfeited) in Washington. Abandonment requires evidence of intent to abandon and nonuse of a water right. Five years of successive nonuse of a right without good cause results in relinquishment of that right.

Adjudication and Federal Reserved Water Rights

A general water rights adjudication (of surface water or ground water or both) is initiated in Washington by petition of an individual or by the Department of Ecology. The adjudication requires that a record be compiled of all known persons claiming the right to divert water on a given source and that a map be prepared showing the boundaries of the water body.[37] These papers are filed with the county superior court, and claimants are then summoned to provide testimony to a water referee.

The water referee issues a report recommending confirmation of rights, priorities, and quantification to the court. The court then holds a hearing on objections to the referee's report and ultimately issues a decree listing the rights of record and their characteristics. This decision may be appealed.

Protecting Washington's Public Water Resources in the Twenty-first Century

Water Planning and Management.

One of the important functions of the Department of Ecology is data gathering and management. This includes hydrographic surveys of stream flows, dam and reservoir data, aquifer characteristics, and location, completion, and pumping rates for permitted wells.

Many regions of the state have also established Ground Water Management Advisory Committees to facilitate the development of ground water management programs. These may include definitions of ground water resources in a given region and plans for present and future allocation, conservation, and quality protection.

Conservation and Prevention of Waste.

State law prohibits the waste of water. Court cases have determined that water use must be through reasonably efficient means. Conservation is addressed in several different ways by Washington water law. State bond funds are available to public irrigation systems for water-saving improvements. Those receiving state financial assistance for construction or expansion of water sources or acquisition of new sources must develop a water supply plan using specific guidelines and implement the plan if it is cost-effective.

Ground water basins may be specially designated to protect them from overdraft. Guidelines have been developed for municipal water conservation. These are used for the development of coordinated water system plans of public utilities. A system of "trust water rights" was established whereby the department may subsidize water conservation projects in exchange for rights to the amount of water conserved through the project. Trust rights can be obtained through purchase or by other means. They can be used to support minimum flows or for irrigation but cannot be used in a manner that impairs existing rights.

Instream Flow.

Washington has established instream flows for rivers and streams in a number of state watercourses. These flows are specifically described in instream resources protection programs in the Washington Administrative Code. The programs established minimum flows for wildlife, fish, aesthetic, scenic, and other environmental values. These appropriations were given a priority date according to the date of their establishment.

Water Quality.

Unlike most other western states, Washington's water allocation and water quality protection programs are both administered by the Department of Ecology. Water use applications may be denied or made conditional if water quality may be affected by the proposed use. Water quality may also be considered a criterion in determining minimum stream flows and lake levels.

Public Interest Criteria.

These criteria are considered when new water use permits are being reviewed.[38]

WYOMING

First Things First: What's the System?

Wyoming is a prior appropriation state with water rights procedures established in state law and court decisions. Primary authority for the appropriation, distribution, and management of water in Wyoming rests with the state engineer.

A Board of Control, consisting of four water division superintendents and the state engineer, also plays an important role in water appropriation in Wyoming.

Who to Contact

The Wyoming state engineer is responsible for water rights.

Wyoming State Engineer
Herschler Building, 4-E
Cheyenne, WY 82002
(307) 777-7354

Ground Water (307) 777-6163
Surface Water (307) 777-6475
Board of Control (307) 777-6178
FAX: (307) 777-5451

How to Get a New Water Right in Wyoming

The only way to establish a new ground water or surface water right in Wyoming is to file application with the state engineer.

To obtain a new surface water right in Wyoming, an application form, filing fee, and certified map must be filed with the state engineer's office.[39] The date of filing becomes the priority date for the water right should it be approved. The application is reviewed for completeness to determine whether it should be accepted. If it is accepted, staff review it to ensure that the proposed use won't impair the value of existing rights or harm the public welfare.

The application is then given to the state engineer. Upon consideration, conditions or limitations may be imposed to protect prior water rights, define the extent of the proposed uses and places of use, and address other issues. Upon approval by the state engineer, the application becomes a permit. The final outcome may be appealed to the Board of Control if the state engineer's decision is disputed by the applicant.

The permittee may be granted up to five years to complete the construction and apply the water to beneficial use. If more time is needed, a request for an extension must be filed. Upon showing due diligence, additional time may be granted. The permittee is required to submit a notice of completion of construction and beneficial use.

Upon receipt of all necessary notices, the Board of Control prepares a proof and conveys it to the water division superintendent for field inspection and verification of completion. After field inspection, the proof is advertised and public comment is received. If protests are made, a public hearing may be held. Once this process is complete, the proof is given to the Board of Control. If the proof is accepted, a Certificate of Appropriation or Certificate of Construction (for reservoirs) is granted, finalizing the water right process. Such water rights are then said to have adjudicated status.

The process for acquiring a ground water right in Wyoming is similar to that required to obtain a surface water right. An application and fee payment are submitted to the state engineer. The date of acceptance of the application becomes the priority date for the right.

The application is reviewed for completeness and accuracy. It is then evaluated to ensure that the planned use doesn't impair the value of existing rights or harm the public welfare.[40]

When the review is complete, the state engineer considers the application. Conditions or limitations may be imposed to protect prior water rights, to better define the extent of the proposed water use, or to address other issues. The application is permitted upon approval. A ground water permittee may also be granted up to five years to complete construction and put the water to beneficial use. Once construction is completed (including well installation), the permittee must file a statement of completion and description of the well. This filing completes the process for stock and domestic wells.

Other Important Things to Know

Before a person holding a water right or permit changes the place or purpose of water use, he/she must petition to do so. Changes in point of diversion, means of conveyance, or other permitted facility or water use are initiated by a petition to the state engineer, if the water right is unadjudicated, or to the Board of Control, if the water right is adjudicated. A public hearing may be required. Changes are allowed if the quantity of transferred water does not exceed historic use, diversion, or consumptive rates; does not decrease the amount of historic returns; and does not impair other rights.

A water right is considered a property right in Wyoming. As such, water use is attached to the lands or to the place of use specified. Storage rights (to waters from a reservoir) are held by the owner of record unless a secondary permit is filed that attaches a specified amount of stored water to a specified place of use for a specific purpose. A reservoir may have several "owners," depending on the situation.

Water rights may be lost by abandonment if not used for a period of five consecutive years when water is available. This occurs if a junior appropriator, or in some cases a senior appropriator, brings a declaration of abandonment to the state Board of Control. The state engineer may also seek a finding of abandonment before the Board of Control. Water lost through abandonment returns to the public and is subject to appropriation.

Adjudication and Federal Reserved Water Rights

Most water rights on streams in Wyoming are adjudicated. About one-fifth of the state is currently undergoing a general adjudication, which is determining tribal and federal water rights and integrating them with the water rights that already have been adjudicated by the state.

All ground water rights, other than for stock or domestic uses, must be adjudicated. This requires that the permittee submit proof of appropriation and beneficial use when ground water has been used as specified in the permit. A map prepared by a professional engineer or land surveyor registered to practice in Wyoming must accompany the proof, showing well location and location of water use. A site visit is made by staff of the state engineer's office to accurately describe the actual facility and water use. The proof is then noticed publicly, and protests may be submitted. A public hearing may result if protests are filed. Thereafter the proof goes to the Board of Control for consideration. If approved, the board issues a Certificate of Appropriation of Ground Water, which is recorded with the appropriate county clerk. The water right is then said to have adjudicated status. All decisions of the Board of Control may be appealed to the district court.

Protecting Wyoming's Public Water Resources in the Twenty-first Century

Water Planning and Management.

Wyoming has a Water Development Commission that is responsible for coordinating both water and related land resources planning. Water resource plans may include complete inventories of the resource, demands, and future needs. Stream feasibility studies have been authorized to determine methods and criteria for preserving scenic and recreational quality of rivers and streams.

Conservation and Prevention of Waste.

Conservation methods are to be investigated by those undertaking water planning and water development. Furthermore, the state engineer may ask the attorney general to sue to stop or prevent water waste or loss. Water waste may be a factor in determining ground water control areas. Local water commissioners, who control the day-to-day management of surface water, are required by law to operate irrigation systems to prevent waste.

Instream Flow.

The primary focus of instream flow protection strategies in Wyoming is the protection of fisheries. Only the state may hold a right for instream flows.

The Game and Fish Commission reports annually to the Water Development Commission those specific segments that have the most critical needs. The Water Development Commission files the application for the instream flow right. The Game and Fish Commission then prepares a biological assessment, and the Water Development Commission prepares a hydrologic analysis of the segment. The state engineer then must study the feasibility of the instream flow segment. A required public hearing is held, in which the biological and hydrologic information is presented and public input is accepted. The application is then presented to the state engineer for consideration.

Public Interest Criteria.

Such criteria are not specifically defined in Wyoming water law. However, public interest concerns are taken into account in many administrative decisions and in future planning.

Endnotes

1. Spanish explorer Don Juan de Oñate was following this example when he established an irrigation system in 1598 at San Juan Pueblo in what is now New Mexico.

2. Generally, riparian water rights are not lost by nonuse, a significant difference from prior appropriation rights. However, riparian rights are not without limitation. Riparian landowners are usually obliged to restrain their own uses of water so as not to interfere with others' rights to reasonable use. In addition, individual riparian rights are limited by public rights to the use of surface water resources for navigation, hunting, and fishing.

3. An exception is made when Congress and the federal government are, or will be, parties to a state's general stream adjudication. See "What Are Federal and Tribal Reserved Water Rights?" in Chapter Three for further details.

4. *Pacific Livestock Co. v. Lewis*, 36 S.Ct.637 (1915). "The rights of all may be evidenced by appropriate certificates and public record always readily accessible."

5. *Pacific Livestock Co. v. Lewis*. "The waters may be distributed, under public supervision, among the lawful claimants according to their respective rights."

6. *Pacific Livestock Co. v. Lewis*. "The amount of surplus water or unclaimed water, if any, may be ascertained."

7. See Laurie Potter, "The Public's Role in the Acquisition and Enforcement of Instream Flows," in *Instream Flow Protection in the West*, ed. Lawrence J. MacDonnell, Teresa A. Rice, and Steven J. Shupe (Boulder: University of Colorado School of Law, Natural Resources Law Center, 1989), pp. 41–68.

8. David Getches, *Water Law in a Nutshell* (St. Paul, MN: West Publishing, 1990), p. 122.

9. The public interest in this case meant protecting Mono Lake from degradation and environmental damage resulting from water diversions to the City of Los Angeles. *National Audubon Society v. Superior Court.*

10. See Harrison C. Dunning, "Instream Flows and the Public Trust," in *Instream Flow Protection in the West*, pp. 103–125.

11. Getches, *Water Law in a Nutshell*, p. 136–150.

12. "The doctrine of prior appropriation recognizes a right of junior appropriators in the continuation of stream conditions as they existed at the time of their respective appropriations. *Farmers Highline Canal & Reservoir Co. v. City of Golden* (1954), quoted by Getches, *Water Law in a Nutshell*, p. 164.

13. *The Irrigation Age*, Volumes 9 and 10 (1897).

14. See Tim DeYoung, "Instream Flow Protection in a Water Market State," in *Instream Flow Protection in the West*, pp. 331–356.

15. Alaska's status is according to Article VII, Section 13, of the state constitution and the Alaska Water Use Act, Alaska Statute 46.15.

16. Beneficial use is defined by Alaska statute as water use for the benefit of the individual or the public that is reasonable and consistent with the public interest. Beneficial uses include domestic, municipal, industrial, mining, agricultural, fish and wildlife, recreational, and water quality activities.

17. A significant amount of water is defined in 11 AAC 93.970(14). In general, any use of five hundred gallons per day for more than ten days a year is considered significant.

18. The Phoenix, Prescott, and Tucson Active Management Areas hope to realize their goals for safe yield by the year 2025.

19. Colorado State Constitution, Article XVI, Section 5 and 6; Colorado Revised Statutes, Section 37, Articles 80–92.

20. Water use applications for more than ten cubic feet per second or greater than one thousand acre-feet of water must be publicly noticed in a regional newspaper.

21. The Idaho Supreme Court has broadly defined local public interest to include any locally important factor.

22. Federal claimants include the Nez Perce Tribe, Shoshone-Bannock Tribes of the Fort Hall Indian Reservation, the Shoshone and Paiute Tribes of the Duck Valley Indian Reservation, the Northwest Band of the Shoshoni Nation, the U.S. Department of Justice, National Park Service, U.S. Fish and Wildlife Service, U.S. Department of Agriculture, U.S. Forest Service, Bureau of Reclamation, and Bureau of Land Management.

23. See Sections 85-1-101, 85-1-203 (2), Montana Code Annotated.

24. Before the act was established, state law provided for the establishment of ground water conservation districts. Five still exist in Clay, Fillmore, Hamilton, Seward, and York Counties.

25. 82 O.S. Supp. 1993, §105.1A; and an April 13, 1993, decision of the Oklahoma Supreme Court in the case of *Franco-American Charolaise, Ltd. v. Oklahoma Water Resources Board and City of Ada* gave riparian water right holders significant protection. Important questions remain to be clarified regarding the implications of this decision. 820 S. Supp. 1995, §105.1A limits riparian use to domestic use and extinguishes future riparian right claims. The *Franco* case differs from the legislation by offering significant protection to riparians.

26. The proportionate share is that percentage of the total yield of the basin equal to the percentage of land overlying the basin that is owned or leased by the applicant. If a hydrologic survey has not been completed to determine the maximum annual yield, the board may issue a temporary permit allowing the withdrawal of two acre-feet per acre owned or leased.

27. The 1.5-million-acre county contains parts of the Arkansas River and Keystone and Kaw Reservoirs, all of the Hulah and Skiatook Lakes, and a scattering of municipal lakes. Considerable ground water resources are also stored in alluvium and terrace deposits of the Arkansas River and the Vamoosa Formation.

28. 82 O.S. Supp. 1993, §105.12, 1020.9, and 1020.15.

29. 82 O.S. 1991, §1451 et seq.

30. Oklahoma Administrative Code, Section 785:45-5-25.

31. OAC 785:20-5-5.

32. Domestic uses are defined as the use of eighteen gallons of water per minute or less on an average daily basis with a peak use of no more than twenty-five gallons of water per minute. Examples of domestic use in South Dakota are (1) drinking, washing, sanitary, and culinary uses by an individual or household; (2) irrigation of a noncommercial garden, trees, and so on, not exceeding one acre in size; (3) stock watering; and (4) use in schools, parks, and public recreation areas not exceeding eighteen gallons per minute.

33. An exception is that no permit is required of a landowner who constructs a dam and reservoir that impounds no more than two hundred acre-feet on a nonnavigable stream, as long as the water is used only for livestock and domestic purposes. If the water from such a structure is used for any other purposes, a permit is required. Certain aquaculture operations using marine water sources are not permitted but must register.

34. Examples of environmental impacts might be degradation of water quality, instream flow impacts, reduction of overall flow to the bays and estuaries, and damage to fish and wildlife habitat.

35. The proof of appropriation must be prepared by a licensed engineer or land surveyor. It verifies the quantity of water that has actually been developed, the extent of use, exact location of the diversion point, and other related information.

36. The statement of proof must indicate (1) exactly which facilities and equipment are being operated, (2) the capacity of the diversion or withdrawal, (3) how much water has been beneficially used, (4) for what purpose the water is being used, (5) where the water is being used, and (6) that all conditions of the permit have been met.

37. Between 1967 and 1974, claimants of surface water uses initiated before 1917 and ground water uses begun before 1945 were required to file a statement of claim for a vested water right. Failure to file such a claim is considered to be a relinquishment of the right. A registry of these vested claims is kept by the Department of Ecology. Final determination as to the validity and quantification of these claims occurs during an adjudication.

38. Such considerations are supported by the Washington legislature as follows: "Allocation of waters among potential uses and users shall be based generally on the securing of the maximum net benefits for the people of the state. Maximum net benefits shall constitute total benefits less costs including opportunities lost."

39. The map must be certified by a Wyoming registered professional engineer or land surveyor (except for stock reservoirs and special applications).

40. An application for a well yielding more than twenty-five gallons of water per minute located in a ground water control area must receive a favorable recommendation by the control area advisory board and be advertised in a newspaper of general circulation in the area of water appropriation.

Glossary

Abandonment—Generally refers to the surrender, relinquishment, or cession of property or of rights. Applied to water rights, defined as an intentional relinquishment of a known right to use water by virtue of nonuse.

Acequia—A Spanish word used in the Southwest to mean a community irrigation ditch or canal.

Acre-foot—The quantity of water required to cover one acre of land to a depth of one foot, which is equivalent to 325,851 gallons of water.

Adjudication—A formal judicial proceeding to determine the extent and validity of a water right.

Appropriation—A grant of authority from a state entity to divert, store, or use the public waters of the state. The word *appropriation* is often used interchangeably with the terms *water right* and *permit*.

Appropriation Doctrine—The system of western water law pertaining to the first-in-time right of taking or diverting water from a watercourse and applying it to a beneficial use.

Appropriator—A person who takes water from a watercourse and applies it to a beneficial use.

Aquifer—A saturated underground geologic formation of rock or other porous material capable of storing water and transmitting it to wells or springs.

Area of Origin Protection—Refers to law, regulation, or policy that provides some measure of protection for a region from which an interbasin water transfer is made.

Basin of Origin—The river basin in which surface waters naturally occur.

Beneficial Use—The use of water for the benefit of the appropriator, other persons, or the public, defined more specifically within each state's water law. It may include (but is not limited to) water used for agriculture (including stock water), domestic, fish and wildlife, industrial, mining, municipal, power, and recreational uses.

Call the River—To make a request or demand that water right holders on a watercourse appropriate water only in accordance with their priority date ranking.

Certificated Water Right—An official, written assurance that the necessary requirements to perfect or finalize a water right have been completed (e.g., diversion and beneficial use).

Compensation—See *Just Compensation.*

Condemnation—The process of taking private property for public use through the power of eminent domain. The Fifth Amendment to the U.S. Constitution requires that just compensation be paid.

Conditional Permit—A water use permit that is dependent upon or granted subject to a condition. For example, a temporary permit may authorize water use for a specific quantity of water in a specified place for a specified time period and under specified conditions.

Conjunctive Management—Integrated management and use of two or more water resources, such as an aquifer and a surface water body.

Conjunctive Use—The integrated use and management of hydrologically connected ground water and surface water.

Conservation—Water-saving methods that serve to increase water supplies by decreasing demands for water.

Consumptive Use—Water withdrawn from a supply that, because of absorption, transpiration, evaporation, or incorporation in a product, is not returned directly to a surface water or ground water supply; hence, water that is lost for immediate further use.

Cubic Feet per Second (cfs)—A standard unit of measure for flowing water. One cfs is equal to 448.8 gallons per minute.

Decree—The judgment of a court, an official order, or settlement.

De minimis—Derived from the Latin phrase *De minimis non curat lex,* meaning that the law does not care for, or take notice of, very small or trifling matters. De minimis water uses are those considered by law too insignificant to notice.

Depletion—The withdrawal of water from surface or ground water reservoirs at a rate greater than the rate of replenishment.

Ditch Rider—Popular name for a water commissioner or local person who is responsible for overseeing water allocation among all water users and for enforcing the priority system on a given watercourse.

Diversion—The removal of water from a natural watercourse by canal, pipe, well, or other conduit for transfer to another watercourse or for application on the land; also called withdrawal.

Drainage Basin—The land area from which water drains into a river; also called watershed or river basin (see *River Basin*).

Duty of Water—The amount of water necessary, and economically used, to successfully grow crops without unnecessary water loss or waste.

Eminent Domain—The right of government to acquire private property for public use, even from an unwilling owner, upon payment of just compensation to the owner.

Enforce—To put something such as a law into effect. Water rights enforcement generally refers to allocating water resources in strict accordance with priority dates associated with each water user's water right, in accordance with terms and conditions specified.

Evapotranspiration—Water dissipated to the atmosphere by evaporation from moist soil and plant transpiration.

Floodplain—The land bordering a river that is subject to flooding during any given period of time.

Flow Rate—The speed or rate at which water is taken from a watercourse or the speed at which it flows past a point (e.g., gallons per hour or minute, cubic feet per second).

Forfeiture—The loss of a water right due to nonuse for a specified time period; varies by state. Can occur involuntarily.

General Stream Adjudication—Involves a judicial proceeding to determine the extent and validity of all water rights within a given geographic area (e.g., one or more river basins or statewide).

Ground Water—Water that occurs beneath the land surface and fills the pore spaces of the rock material in which it occurs; also called percolating water (see *Percolating Waters*).

Ground Water Mining—The withdrawal of water from an aquifer at rates in excess of net recharge or replenishment. Eventually, the underground supply will be exhausted or will not be economically feasible to pump.

Hybrid System—The popular terminology for water allocation systems that rely on both prior appropriation and riparian systems.

Hydrologic Cycle—The circulation of water from the sea, through the atmosphere, to the land and then back to the sea by overland and subterranean routes or directly back into the atmosphere by evaporation and transpiration.

Hydrology—The science of the behavior of water in the atmosphere, on the earth's surface, and underground.

Instream Flow—The amount of water remaining in a stream, without diversion, that is required to maintain a particular aquatic environment or water use.

Instream Use—Use of water that does not require withdrawal or diversion from its natural watercourse; for example, the use of water for navigation, recreation, hydroelectric production, and support of fish and wildlife habitat. A nonconsumptive use of water.

Interbasin Transfer—The physical transfer of water from one watershed to another.

International Water Treaty—An agreement between the United States and a foreign nation dealing with a water resource involving both nations. Such treaties supersede state law. The United States has treaties with Mexico and Canada relating to shared water resources.

Interstate Water Compact—An agreement between two or more states dealing with competing demands for a water resource beyond the legal authority of one state alone to solve. Such agreements require the consent of Congress.

Just Compensation—Compensation that is fair to both the owner and the public when property is taken for public use through condemnation or eminent domain. Criteria applied may include the market value of the property and the resulting damage to the remaining property of the owner.

Litigate—To engage in legal proceedings.

Mainstem—The principal watercourse of a river, excluding any tributaries.

Make Call—See *Call the River*.

Mayordomo—A Spanish word that is used in the Southwest to identify the local person who is responsible for overseeing water allocation and maintenance of the water conveyance systems. A southwestern synonym for water commissioner or ditch rider.

Navigable Waters—Those waters capable of supporting commerce.

Nonconsumptive Use—Use of water with return to the stream or watercourse of substantially the same amount of water as withdrawn; a use in which only insignificant amounts of water are lost.

Nonpoint Source Pollution—Diffuse, overland runoff containing pollutants; pollution discharges from over a wide land area, not from one location.

Percolating Waters—Waters that pass through the ground beneath the surface of the earth without any definite channel and that do not form a part of the body or flow, surface or subterranean, of any watercourse. May be rainwater slowly infiltrating through soil or water seeping through banks or the bed of a stream, but these waters have left the flow of the stream so that they no longer may be characterized as a part of the stream flow.

Perfected Water Right—A completed or fully executed water right. A water right is said to have been perfected when all terms and conditions associated with it have been fully accomplished (e.g., a diversion has been completed and the water has been put to beneficial use).

Practicably Irrigable Acreage—A standard used to determine the extent of a federal reserved water right on Indian reservations that was established to "transform the Indians into farmers." The practicably irrigable acreage (PIA) standard was established in *Arizona v. California* (1963). A more recent court case involving a general stream adjudication in the Big Horn Basin, Wyoming (1988), applied a two-part test to determine PIA lands: those physically capable of sustained irrigation and those irrigable at a reasonable cost.

Precipitation—Any form of rain, snow, or hail falling to the earth's surface.

Preference System—State laws or constitutional provisions that establish a preference ranking for certain types of water use over others. Commonly rank domestic or municipal use as the highest use, agricultural use second, and industrial and mining uses third.

Prior Appropriation Doctrine—The western system of water appropriation that establishes water rights based on the priority of water use—that is, an individual's right to a specific quantity of water depends on when the use began. The first person to use the water from a source established the first right, the second person established the next right, and so on. During dry years, the person with the first right (senior right) has the first chance to use the available water. The holder of the second right (a junior right) would have the second use, and so on. (See *Appropriation Doctrine*.)

Priority Date—The officially recognized date associated with a water right. It is determined by each state in a somewhat unique fashion. Relative to other rights, the priority date may make a water right senior (predating other rights) or junior (subordinate to other rights).

Property Right—A generic term that refers to any type of right to specific property, whether it is personal or real property, tangible or intangible. For example, a landowner has a property right to use water attached to his or her land.

Recharge—The addition of water to an aquifer by natural infiltration or by artificial injection through wells.

Relicensing—The process of renewing a license previously issued by the federal government (commonly involving the Federal Energy Regulatory Commission) to operate a hydroelectric facility.

Reserved Water Right—A water right recognized by judicial decision to have been created under federal law by a federal reservation of land in an amount sufficient to meet the purposes of the reservation, whether for Indian reservations or for other federal reservations of lands. The right is not lost by nonuse, and its priority date is the date the land was set aside.

Reservoir—A pond, lake, aquifer, or basin, either natural or artificial, in which water is stored or controlled.

Return Flow—The portion of withdrawn water that is not consumed by evapotranspiration and that returns to its source or another body of water.

Right to Capture—The common law rule known as the right to capture governs ground water law in Texas. The rule says that landowners have a right to take for use or sale all the water that they can capture from below their land.

Riparian Doctrine—The system of water law based on English common law allowing landowners adjoining lakes and rivers to withdraw "reasonable amounts" of water so long as downstream landowners are not unreasonably damaged.

Riparian Rights—The water rights of landowners adjacent to rivers and streams.

River Basin—The area from which water drains to a single point; in a natural basin, the drainage area contributing flow to a given point on a stream.

Salvage—Water available for beneficial use because an existing permittee or water right holder does not use his/her full appropriation due to application of water-saving practices.

Severance—The act of severing or separating. In most western states, water rights are considered attached to the land on which they are used. When land is sold, water rights automatically transfer with the land to the new owner, unless such rights are specifically severed from the land by deed.

Storage Right—The authority from a responsible state entity to impound water in a reservoir.

Surface Water—Water above the surface of the land, including (but not limited to) lakes, rivers, streams, diffused surface water, wastewater, floodwater, and ponds.

Temporary Transfer—A transfer of a water right from one purpose to another for a designated period of time.

Transbasin—Typically, transportation of water from one river basin to another river basin.

Transfer—The act of transferring a water right from one person to another. Most states require that some formal notice or filing be made with an appropriate state agency so that the transaction is recorded officially, and the new owner is noted in the official water rights record.

Usufructuary Right—A water right holder's authority to divert and use a certain amount of water.

Vested Water Right—A fully executed or finalized appropriative right to use state water for a beneficial purpose.

Water Administration—A broad term referring to the collective role of defined state agencies to implement state and federal water law, commonly through the development and implementation of appropriate regulations. This role can include oversight, approval, and enforcement responsibilities.

Water Bank—A mechanism for holding water for eventual use. Several western states use water banks of different varieties. For example, since the 1930s, farmers in Idaho have marketed water through the Upper Snake Water Bank. Using three reservoirs (American Falls, Jackson Lake, and Palisades), irrigators have been able to maintain large water supplies as a hedge against drought. Another type of bank was established by the Kern County Water Agency of Central California with the California State Department of Water Resources. It involved purchase of 46,000 acres of land to develop an underground storage facility. During years of surplus, the underground water is sold by the state to parties who need it. A third example is the East Columbia Basin Water Bank operated by the East Columbia Basin Irrigation District. The bank leases water that has been salvaged as a result of conversion to sprinkler irrigation and changes in cropping patterns.

Water Commissioner—A person whose job is to make sure the water of each stream under his or her control is distributed in proper quantities at the right times to those who are authorized to receive it. May also be called a ditch rider or *mayordomo*. May be elected or hired by local water users or appointed by a state authority such as the state engineer or a judge.

Water Permit—A state license to appropriate water for a beneficial purpose.

Water Reservation—A water right granted by a state entity (commonly to public entities and on behalf of the public) for existing or future beneficial uses or for maintenance of a minimum flow, level, or quality of water.

Water Right—A legal right to divert state waters for a beneficial purpose.

References

Black, Henry Campbell. 1990. *Black's Law Dictionary*, 6th ed. St. Paul, MN: West Publishing.

Bokum, Consuelo, Vickie Gabin, and Paige Morgan. 1992. *Living Within Our Means: A Water Management Policy for New Mexico in the 21st Century*. Santa Fe: New Mexico Environmental Law Center.

Dunbar, Robert G. 1983. *Forging New Rights in Western Waters*. Lincoln: University of Nebraska Press.

Emmons, David M. 1971. *Garden in the Grasslands*. Lincoln: University of Nebraska Press.

A Farmer's Guide to Water Rights. 1993. Kearney: Nebraska Water Users, Inc.

Getches, David H. 1990. *Water Law in a Nutshell*. St. Paul, MN: West Publishing.

Getches, David H. et al. 1991. *Controlling Water Use: The Unfinished Business of Water Quality Protection*. Boulder: University of Colorado School of Law, Natural Resources Law Center.

Johnson, Norman K. 1987. *The Doctrine of Prior Appropriation and the Changing West*. Western States Water Council.

————. 1992. *Western State Water Right Permitting Procedures*. Western States Water Council.

Kaiser, Ronald A. 1986. *Handbook of Texas Water Law: Problems and Needs*. College Station: Texas Water Resources Institute.

MacDonnell, Lawrence J., Teresa A. Rice, and Steven J. Shupe. 1989. *Instream Flow Protection in the West*. Boulder: University of Colorado School of Law, Natural Resources Law Center.

Reisner, Marc, and Sarah Bates. 1990. *Overtapped Oasis: Reform or Revolution for Western Water*. Washington, DC: Island Press.

Shupe, Steven J. 1990. *Water Rights Decisions in the Western States: Upgrading the System for the 21st Century*. Western Water Policy Project Discussion Series, no. 4. Boulder: University of Colorado School of Law, Natural Resources Law Center.

Stegner, Wallace. 1992. *Where the Bluebird Sings to the Lemonade Springs.* London: Penguin Books.

U.S. Department of the Interior. *National Water Summary 1987—Hydrologic Events and Water Supply and Use.* 1990. Water Supply Paper 2350, U.S. Geological Survey. Washington, DC: U.S. Government Printing Office.

Webb, Walter Prescott. 1959. *The Great Plains.* Waltham, MA: Blaisdell Publishing.

Wilkinson, Charles F. 1989. "Aldo Leopold and Western Water Law: Thinking Perpendicular to the Prior Appropriation Doctrine." *Land and Water Law Review* (University of Wyoming) 24(1): 93–1010.

————. 1992. *The Eagle Bird: Mapping a New West.* New York: Vintage Books.